Maggie Wright

African Grey Parrots

Everything About History, Care,
Nutrition, Handling, and Behavior

Filled with Full-color Photographs
and Illustrations

2 CONTENTS

UNDERSTANDING THE NATURE OF AFRICAN GREY PARROTS

"Why does my African grey scream when I leave the room? Why does it act nervous when I bring in the groceries? Why does it act shy when I bring over my friends?" These are examples of the many questions we get from readers of The Grey Play Round Table, a magazine dedicated to African grey care.

Wild by Nature

Based on six years of answering questions and publishing the grey magazine, I've learned that the more one understands the "wild nature"of African grey parrots, the better one will understand how to work with them. In this book, we will explore some of these wild instincts. Then we will discuss how this behavior translates into the home.

Not Little Children

Greys are most noted for their intelligence and talking abilities. Dr. Irene Pepperberg of the University of Arizona and her grey research subject, Alex, have proven the intelligence potential of these parrots. Alex can perform many of the same cognitive tasks as chimpanzees, dolphins, and four-year-old children.

African greys are intelligent, sensitive creatures.

He can name and request over 50 items, identify seven colors and five shapes, count up to six, and understand the concepts "same," "different," "bigger," and "smaller." Alex has also been successful at creating his own labels for certain objects, such as "banerry" for apple and "cork nut" which is an almond in a shell.

Most grey owners have stories about how their parrots have shocked them with appropriate language. One night my friend Eva Huebner told her grey Domino that he was going to bed if he didn't stop chewing on the sofa. Domino stopped chewing for a moment, then said, "So what." My own African grey, Merlin Tewillager, was jealous of my other grey, Sweet Pea, when Pea first came to live with us. One day, while I was cuddling Pea, Merle said to Sweet Pea, "Yick! You're lucky!!!"

Their uncannily appropriate and cognitive communication abilities have led many owners to view them like little children. But they are *not* children. They are incredibly intelligent wild animals with different viewpoints. Even though their thought processes may appear logically similar, they sense things differently. They do not share the same perspectives as humans.

Not Domesticated Animals

It takes thousands of generations to domesticate an animal. Domestication is defined as a process by which a population of animals becomes adapted to man. For example, wolves became dogs by breeding the tamest ones. After generations of selective breeding, their personalities and instincts were altered to get along with man. Although no one knows when this domestication process began, some sources believe that the first encounter of taming the wolf may have been as early as the late glacial period, approximately 14,000 B.C. (Boessneck, 1985).

In contrast to the dog, current captive-bred parrots are, at most, only one or two generations removed from the wild. This means that domestically bred greys are still wild animals with millions of years of genetic programming from their wild ancestors.

The Learning Process

Bird behavior can be classified into two parts: instinctive and learned. Instinct is the genetic programming, or hard wiring, that a bird is born with. It is a specie's way of surviving through programmed behavior over generations of natural selection. However, birds must also be able to adapt their behavior, in order to survive in changing environments. Therefore, both instinctive and learned behaviors are important.

Many acquired skills are developed by utilizing both instinct and learned behavior. For example, flying is instinctive. But successfully maneuvering and landing is learned by practice and observation. Preening is also instinctive. However, perfecting the art of preening is also learned by observation and practice.

Associative Learning

"Associative learning"[1] is one form of learned behavior. It is a process whereby the chick learns skills by closely observing its parents or other older birds.

Wild African grey chicks live in small family units. They continue to learn skills from their parents until at least one year of age (see Rearing of the Young, page 9). However, domestically-bred chicks are removed from their parents at six weeks of age or younger. Therefore, in contrast to their wild cousins, they do not get the additional "associative learning" from their parents. Instead, they imprint on humans. They learn to eat their food from a bowl instead of foraging. They learn to play with a toy in the cage, rather than another bird.

However, when domestically-bred grey chicks are faced with stressful situations, they revert to their instinctive responses. But again, they lack the "associative learning" on how to handle these situations. For example, the fear of a predator is instinctive. But the strategy for protecting themselves is a learned skill. Wild chicks are taught who their predators are by their parents, as well as strategies for protecting themselves, such as freezing or flying away. In contrast, domestically-bred greys have the instinctive fear, but they lack the learned behavior of who the predators are and how to protect themselves. Therefore, anyone that surprises them, or is too aggressive with them, may trigger that instinctive fear. As a result, many have turned phobic of their owners in fearful situations. They associate their owners as being "predators" (see Rehabilitating Greys). Phobic and other situations can be avoided, simply by understanding these instinctive responses and learning how to work with them.

Importance of the Flock

According to Tony Juniper and Mike Parr in their book, *Parrots: A Guide to Parrots of the World*, wild greys live mainly in lowland tropical forests and mangroves. They roost (sleep) in large flocks, ranging from several hundred to thousands of birds. The roost sites are in tall palms or trees located either near water or on islands in the middle of rivers. At dawn they disperse into smaller flock groups. They fly long distances to forage in fruit trees in mangroves and along savanna woodlands.

The main reason birds "flock" is for protection. In his book, *The Lives of Birds,* ornithologist Lester Short says that predators like hawks tend to avoid attacking flocks in the air because at the high speeds they fly, they could break a wing, just by touching one of the prey birds. Thus, many flocks close up and fly erratically to confuse the attackers. Furthermore, feeding in flocks allows individual birds to spend more time looking for and eating food, and less time looking out for predators. They have more eyes scanning the territory.[2]

Depending on their habitat, life circumstances, and territorial competition, parrot species adapt and create different social flock systems. For example, many Central and South American (New World) parrots, such as macaws, amazons, and conures, congregate together in "multispecies" flocks. But greys in Africa associate only with other greys in "single-species" flocks.[3] Some aviculturists believe the New World parrots form multispecies flocks because they face more competition for nest cavities and food, which forces them to intermingle across species.

Another difference between greys and New World parrots is that most New World parrots pair off from their flocks to breed. But, according to Mr. Juniper and Mr. Parr, some greys breed near one another in loose colonies of up to several hundred pairs. This means they are together all the time.

Although there is little research on the structure and social interactions within wild grey flocks, we have anecdotal information as breeders observe their wild-caught greys in captivity. Grey breeder Pamela Clark describes her wild-caught breeding greys as being so sensitive and in tune with each other that they appear to operate as a "one-group-mind." She explains that they sit together, quietly and cautiously. They are always observing. They are conservative and watchful. They appear to have an affinity for one another.[4]

Feeding Habits

Wild African greys eat flowers, fruits, seeds, stems, leaves, roots, and soil. Diana May, a Ph.D. student advised by Dr. Pepperberg, began researching the wild habits of greys in the Congo Basin rainforest in 1995. In the Dzanga-Sangha Reserve, located in southwestern Central African Republic, she observed groups of 30 to 300 Congo greys ground feeding on plants in Dzanga Bai, a muddy forest clearing.[5]

Baby greys in captivity are removed from their parents at six weeks of age or younger.

In 1997, May and Carolyn Bentley (an undergraduate student) observed groups of up to 800 Congo Greys at a marsh clearing in the Lobéké Reserve, located in southeastern Cameroon. They observed the parrots not only feeding on plants, but also eating soil. Soil-eating is a behavior known as geophagy.[6]

Dr. May describes how the parrots arrived every day in singles, pairs, and small groups of up to six, eventually forming larger flocks.[7] She notes, "several individuals arrive at a favorite tree, usually a tree that is barren of leaves and located at the edge of the forest clearing. They will perch in the tree, preen, climb, vocalize, interact, and in general, cycle through a complex behavioral repertoire. A few minutes later, a few more arrive. They also join in the activity. . . . Within the hour, the tree becomes filled with grey parrots that together produce a cacophony of whistles, squawks, shrieks, chirps, and other sounds."[8] They descend to ground-forage in waves. The entire flock is never on the ground at once.

These observations are significant because they are the first scientific visual evidence of ground-foraging. Dr. May observed the parrots spending approximately 40 minutes per day on the ground, eating plants and soil. According to Dr. May, the soil in Cameroon is rich in minerals.[9] The only other reference to ground-foraging is in Joseph Forshaw's book, *Parrots of the World*, which notes quartz occasionally being found in stomach contents.[10] The only way in which they could have eaten quartz was to feed on the ground.

Types of Greys

African greys originate from western and central Africa, ranging from northern Angola to Guinea. There are two general types. The Congo African grey (*Psittacus erithacus erithacus*) is the largest, usually 16 ounces (450 g) and over in weight and 12 to 14 inches (32–36 cm) in length. It is gray in color with a solid black beak and bright red tail. The second type, the Timneh African grey (*Psittacus erithacus timneh*) is smaller in size, about 10 inches (26 cm) in length and 10.5 ounces (300 g) in weight and over. It is darker in color with a brownish-to-maroon-colored tail and a pinkish or horn-colored upper mandible (beak).

If you hear reference to Ghana, Cameroon, Togo, or Angola greys, they are "street" names for the nominate species, the Congo grey. They refer to the locations from which they came, according to grey breeder Jean Pattison. She says that the Congo first exported African greys. However, when they ceased exporting them, the term "Congo grey" remained a generic label for any bright red-tailed parrot.[11]

Sexual Differences

Like most parrots, greys are monomorphic. This means the sexes look alike to humans. Although some aviculturists claim to be able to tell the differences by sight, the DNA test is the most accurate. It is a simple blood test conducted by an avian veterinarian. In general, the male Congo tends to be darker gray in color, with a flat square head and larger beak relative to head size. The hen tends to be lighter in color, with a more rounded, dainty head and smaller beak. It is more difficult to tell differences between the Timneh sexes.

Breeding

The breeding season in Africa varies by locality, but it appears to coincide with the dry season. Pairs nest in trees that have deep cavities and are high off the ground. The hen lays three to five eggs over a period of a few days. The male feeds her as she incubates them for about 30 days. They both feed the nestlings once they hatch. They act in tandem as a couple with separate behaviors to protect and raise their young and to preserve the species. The male is the protector of the nest and territory. The hen is the nurturer of the young.

Since this genetic patterning remains intact in domestically raised greys, the male tends to be a little biting and aggressive in breeding season. The hen tends to be a little needy, although more even-tempered. However, as a species, they are known to be calmer than most territorially-aggressive parrot species during mating season. Some grey owners have not noticed any changes in their grey compan-

Wild Congo greys eat plants and soil (Bolou Savanna, Lobéké Reserve, Cameroon).

ions' behavior at all. Outside of breeding season, it is difficult to detect any differences in their personalities.

Some people believe that domestic male greys prefer women owners and female greys prefer male owners. This is not true. There are many cases where male greys prefer men over women, and the hens prefer female owners. In cases where there are sexual preferences, the reasons may relate to preferring humans of the same sex of a "favored" human, or one with whom they've had a positive early experience, such as a hand feeder. However, there is no generic rule of "opposite sex preferences."

Rearing of the Young

Parrots across the world live in many different habitats. Depending on their circumstances, they adapt their lives in order to survive. This includes how they raise their young. Yellow-naped and Blue-fronted Amazons, for example, have a reputation for being socially quick maturing parrots. Their young receive intense survival training in a short period of time so that they become independent in their flocks when they fledge. By contrast, some parrots

like Galah (Rose-breasted) cockatoos in Australia have longer periods of maturation. The fledglings are kept in large creches, and the parents continue to feed and instruct them.[12] Cockatoo expert Sam Foster theorizes that the amazons mature quicker than the Galahs because there is more competition in South and Central America from other parrot species for food and nest cavities. This forces them to grow up quicker in order to survive.[13]

Congo African greys require longer periods of maturation, similar to the Galahs. They have been observed in small groups of up to six foraging in the trees, and up to eight in the early evenings.[14] It is theorized these small groups may be family units that remain intact until the chicks become independent.[15]

Avian behavior consultant Jane Hallander believes that wild Timneh greys raise their young differently from Congos. She hypothesizes that, similar to some of the New World parrots, Timneh chicks are taught their survival skills in a shorter period. They are prepared to leave their family units approximately six months earlier than the Congos.[16] Her rationale is that as birds become more independent in the flock and learn to get along with others outside the family unit, they tend to vocalize more extensively. For example, Yellow-nape and Blue-fronted Amazons join their flocks when they fledge. They are known to begin talking (phrase-making) in captivity close to the fledging age, as early as three-to-six months old. Timnehs appear to follow the same pattern as the Amazons.

Ms. Hallander conducted an informal survey to analyze vocalization patterns of both companion Congos and Timnehs. Results showed that although many Congos may have said their first words within a few months of age, their phrase-making and appropriate chattering did not start until the parrots were at least 12 to 18 months old. In contrast, the Timnehs began their word chattering earlier, at approximately six months of age. This does not mean Timnehs are smarter or better talkers. They are genetically programmed to mature earlier than their Congo cousins.[17]

Unfortunately, little scientific research has been done to test these hypotheses, but perhaps we will have more definitive information over the next few years.

The Grey Personality

Both Congo and Timneh African greys make wonderful companions. They are good talkers, and besides the differences in appearance and size, their personalities are similar. Overall, they are cautious, sensitive, observant, and intelligent flock animals. They tend to be shyer and more reclusive around strangers (nonflock members) than other parrots. They are also quieter as a whole. But, if there is a sound that attracts them, such as a microwave beep or cockatoo scream, they can be as loud as any parrot, especially if they get a reaction.

They are called the "dweebs" of the parrot world. Their intelligence, observation skills, and talking abilities allow many to manipulate their households. Sometimes they seem so "humanlike." They appear to operate out of their heads, thinking, analyzing, and appropriately speaking.

Although they share many characteristics as a group, their personalities are individual. Some are aggressive and playful. Some are quiet. Some are outgoing and comical. Others are shy. Some are talkative. Others are not. Some are territorial. Others are laid back. Some are standoffish. Others are affectionate.

One Person Birds?

Greys are often called fickle. Many owners have complained that they change their favored human bonds from the one who nurtured them as chicks to another household member. Jane Hallander conducted an informal survey on longtime bonding patterns. The surveyed birds were DNA sexed, at least three years old, domestically bred, and they lived in homes with two or more people. Ms. Hallander found that 63 percent of the male Congo greys changed loyalties between the ages of one and one half and two years of age. They usually switched their loyalties from the primary nurturer to another family member. However, only 16 percent of the female Congo greys switched preferred humans as they matured.[18]

Ms. Hallander concluded that the results "suggest" that if wild Congo greys are raised in close family groups within the flock for an extended period, as it is theorized, then "natural selection" would force them to reject the family unit to find a suitable mate. This would allow them to carry on the gene pool. She said that if the male selects the mate, this would account for the high number of male Congos that reject their original favored humans for another family member.

Ms. Hallander further noted that although parrots may not view their owners as mates, the "instinctive urge" to leave the family group may be strong enough to trigger some domestically-raised greys to reject the favored humans that nurtured them as chicks. They would then select another member of the household that represents the new flock.

In the same survey, none of the Timnehs (neither males nor hens) rejected their favored humans. Perhaps this was because, in the wild, they leave their family units to join their flocks at earlier ages than the Congos (approximately four-to-six months). Therefore, in captivity, they may be moving to their new human homes at the same time that they would have been naturally leaving their families in the wild. Thus, they choose their "permanent favored mates" when they originally choose their humans, either at the breeder's or in the pet store.

The survey was informal. It was not meant to be hard scientific fact; therefore, the information only "suggests" a pattern of behavior. Not all Congo greys, including the males, reject their favored humans. However, if this does happen to you, do not take it personally. You did *not* do anything wrong.

Some aviculturists have misunderstood this rejection. They believe that the parrot rejects the first favored human because that human is perceived by the parrot to be weaker or lower in status than the newly chosen family member. This is not true. It is an instinctive part of the young grey's development. The rejection may not last forever.

Implications

Partial ground feeders: All parrots are prey animals. However, parrots that feed off the ground, in addition to the forest canopy (trees), face even more danger. First, it is more difficult to escape from the ground in a predatory attack. Secondly, it is easier to be seen on the ground by a predator that is flying from above and searching for prey. Third, ground feeders are also vulnerable to being attacked by ground predators.

As a result, ground feeders must be cautious with quick reflexes. They must be keenly observant of quick movements and anything near them that is different. For example, ground predators, such as cats, stalk their prey by sneaking up on them. They slowly move forward, one foot at a time, so that their prey does not notice them until it is too late. A wild grey must be aware of the placement of everything around it because anything that is different or new in its territory could be a ground predator. Or it could be a hawk that is hiding in the trees. This may account for companion greys' cautious nature and nervous reactions to unfamiliar objects and quick movements around them in the home.

Birds of one feather: Greys are single-species flock birds. They are genetically programmed only to associate with others of their kind. When they fly in large flocks, and when they go to the ground in groups, they must look one color. Upon reviewing Diana May's film of wild greys, grey breeder Pamela Clark observed that when the sunlight bounces off their gray and white feathers while flying, and when they flop on the ground to eat, practically huddling on top of one another, it is difficult for any predator to single them out.[19] For their own survival, they cannot accept other species in their flocks that do not look like them. As a result, companion greys are not genetically programmed to deal with the idiosyncrasies and personalities of different parrot species. Some of them may not get along with other parrots. They may either ignore or attack them. This does not mean they will never get

Congo greys (**Psittacus erithacus erithacus**) *have solid black beaks.*

Timneh greys (**Psittacus erithacus timneh**) *have horn-colored beaks.*

along with other species. Nor does it mean that you should have a flock of just grey parrots. However, the socialization process of integrating the different species should be supervised carefully. There are many instances where greys, amazons, and other parrot species get along.

More dependence on the flock: Wild greys appear to be more dependent upon the flock for their own survival than most parrots. As previously discussed, they congregate only with each other. Many breed in loose colonies, instead of separating from the flock. They flop about and huddle close together while feeding on the ground. If one parrot senses danger, the whole flock reacts. Their survival depends on how attuned they are to one another.

Accordingly, in the home, domestic greys are keenly sensitive and "tuned in" to the thoughts, feelings, and emotional health of their "human flock." If there is a problem in the family flock, such as an owner's sadness over a relationship that has broken up or anger and frustration over a job that is not going well, the grey picks up on it. Even though it may not understand the ramifications, it senses that something is wrong with the flock. It senses there is danger. Helping your grey feel safe and secure is your most important job.

Maturation process: Many greys have a reputation for being neurotic and nervous. Some aviculturists believe this is due to the ways in which they are being bred in captivity. They are not raised by their parents. They are thrust at their human flocks immediately after being weaned. We've discussed the theory that wild Congo chicks remain with their parents

for long periods of instruction. Accordingly, they may also require longer periods of development and instruction before they are ready to join their human flocks. Think about what it would be like if a human baby were "bred" or brought up until the crawling stage. Then its parents left it alone without any further parental guidance.

In an attempt to replicate breeding in the wild, Pamela Clark utilizes a "nanny bird" system. Two of her Congo greys, Rollo and Sister Woman, assist in raising the chicks. They serve as role models. They nurture the babies. Rollo sometimes "spars" with the males which helps to build self-confidence. They go to their human flocks when they are approximately five months old.[20]

Some aviculturists believe that Timnehs are calmer because they mature faster than Congos. They are genetically programmed to learn all they need to survive in a shorter period of time. Other quick maturing parrots, such as amazons, do not exhibit the nervous tendencies and other phobic behaviors that some of the slower maturing Congo greys and Rose-breasted cockatoos experience, when they are not properly nurtured.

It has often been said that African greys are one of the easiest species to breed. However, I disagree. They may be easy physically to brood. But it is difficult to help them develop into the secure, confident creatures that they become in the wild. We must research and understand how they are raised in the wild, so that we can replicate this process in captivity. I do not recommend that anyone consider breeding African greys until we know more about their wild habits. For this reason, breeding will not be discussed in this book.

Conservation, Aviculture, and Legislation

Wild African greys face many dangers. In addition to threats of habitat loss, their "pet potential" popularity has made them highly sought after by trappers. It has been illegal since 1993 (Wild Bird Conservation Act, signed October 1992) to import wild greys into the United States; however, they continue to be exported from Africa to other countries worldwide. In fact, they face potential extinction in some African countries, such as Nigeria, because they are being illegally smuggled at such a rapid rate. CITES (Convention on International Trade in Endangered Species), African governments, and

other groups are working hard to eliminate illegal poaching and to design sound control systems for legally trapping and exporting greys. However, the task is proving difficult. Many concerned aviculturists cite political and economic instability, poor enforcement, pressure from wealthy importers, and general corruption as some of the contributing factors. The bottom line is money. Each parrot can sell for at least $500 on the international trade market.

Many of the poachers come from urban areas. They stake out their territories near forest savanna clearings, and they solicit local villagers to do the trapping. Sometimes, however, villagers stand up to the poachers. The village, Ikodi, located on the southeastern coast of Nigeria, is one example. Ikodi villagers want to protect the grey parrot in its habitat. Their village is locally known as "parrots paradise," and many of the tribes people augment their income by collecting and selling molten grey-red tail feathers that have fallen to the ground. According to a report in the World Parrot Trust magazine, *PsittaScene*, the local Ikodi tribes people stood up to poachers in 1999. The skirmish resulted in the death of two Ikodi youths.[21]

Additionally, excessive wildlife trapping affects ecosystem integrity and wildlife movement. For example, it was discovered that large mammals (such as elephants) only feed at night in three savanna clearings in the Lobéké forest in southeastern Cameroon. But in contrast, they feed regularly during the day in adjacent forests. The difference is that the adjacent forests (Nouabalé-Ndoki National Park and Dzanga-Sangha Dense Forest Reserve) are legally protected from trappers and hunters. The animals restrict their daily feeding habits to avoid being trapped and hunted.[22]

As long as people and countries worldwide are willing to buy smuggled grey parrots, this problem will persist. Many conservationists recommend that ecotourism systems be created in Africa. Similar to the success that Charles Munn has experienced with ecotourism for macaws in Manu Park in Peru, employment of trappers in African ecotourism (such as tour guides and forest guards) could refocus their efforts to conservation.

Grey parrots are not meant for everyone. Anyone lucky enough to have that special bond with one will be converted to the species forever. The following chapters will explore the process for cultivating that special relationship.

[1]Short, Lester L. *The Lives of Birds.* Henry Holt and Company, New York, New York. 1993. p.51.

[2]Short, Lester L. *The Lives of Birds.* Henry Holt and Company; New York, New York. 1993. pp.62-66.

[3]May, D. L. (1998). *The Reproductive Biology and Behavior of Free-living Grey Parrots (Psittacus erithacus) in Africa.* Unpublished technical report (Grant No. AC52), World Wildlife Fund—U.S.

[4]Clark, Pamela. "A Society of Greys." *Grey Play Round Table.* Tewillager Publishing, division of Equatorial Group, Ltd.; Old Chatham, New York; Spring 1999; p. 11.

[5]May, D. L. (1996, Fall). "The Behavior of African Grey Parrots in the Rainforest of the Central African Republic." *PsittaScene.* 8, 8-9.

[6]May, D. L. (1998). *The Reproductive Biology and Behavior of Free-living Grey Parrots (Psittacus erithacus) in Africa.* Unpublished technical report. (Grant No. AC52), World Wildlife Fund—U.S.

Bentley, C. S., May, D. L., and Pepperberg, I. M. (1998). "Food Selection by African Grey Parrots in Cameroon." Poster presented at southwestern and Rocky Mountain Division of the American Association for the Advancement of Science Annual Meeting, May 1998, Grand Junction, Colorado.

[7]May, D. L. Personal correspondence. September, 2000.

[8]May, D. L. "The Behavior of Grey Parrots in the Rainforest of the Central African Republic." *PsittaScene.* 8, 8-9.

[9]Bentley and May, Personal communication, September 2000.

[10]Forshaw, Joseph M. *Parrots of the World.* T.F.H. Publications, Inc. Neptune, New Jersey. 1977. p. 288.

[11]Pattison, Jean. "African Grey Variations." *Grey Play Round Table.* Tewillager Publishing, division of Equatorial Group, Ltd. Old Chatham, New York. Spring 2000, pp. 18-19.

[12]Juniper, Tony, and Mike Parr. *Parrots: A Guide to Parrots of the World.* Yale University Press. New Haven, Connecticut. 1998. p. 275.

[13]Foster, Sam, and Jane Hallander. "Cockatoos and African Greys: Are They Really That Different?" *The Pet Bird Report.* The Pet Bird Council, Inc.; Alameda, California. Volume 8; number 3; issue 41. pp. 16-20.

[14]May, D. L. Personal correspondence. September, 2000.

[15]Foster, Sam, and Jane Hallander. "Cockatoos and African Greys: Are They Really That Different?" *The Pet Bird Report.* The Pet Bird Council, Inc.; Alameda, California. Volume 8; number 3; issue 41. pp. 16-20.

[16]Foster, Sam, and Jane Hallander. "Cockatoos and African Greys: Are They Really That Different?" *The Pet Bird Report.* The Pet Bird Council, Inc.; Alameda, California. Volume 8; number 3; issue 41. pp 16-20.

[17]Hallander, Jane. "Congos and Timnehs: Is There a Difference?" *Grey Play Round Table.* Tewillager Publishing, division of Equatorial Group, LTD; Old Chatham, New York. Spring 1999. pp 4, 17-19.

[18]Foster, Sam, and Jane Hallander. "Cockatoos and African Greys: Are They Really That Different?" *The Pet Bird Report.* Pet Bird Council, Inc.; Alameda, California. Volume 8; number 3; issue 41. pp 16-20.

[19]Clark, Pamela. "A Society of Greys." *Grey Play Round Table.* Tewillager Publishing, a division of the Equatorial Group, LTD. Old Chatham, New York. Spring 1999. p. 24.

[20]Clark, Pamela. "An Innovative Approach to Rearing African Greys," *Grey Play Round Table.* Tewillager Publishing, division of Equatorial Group, Ltd., Old Chatham, New York. Winter 1999. p.14.

[21]Abiodun Raufu, Earth Times News Service. "Smugglers Trap Nigeria's Endangered Grey Parrots to Brink of Extinction." *PsittaScene*: volume 11, No 4, November 1999.

[22]The Lobéké Forest, Southeast Cameroon: Summary of Activities. Period 1988-1995. The Wildlife Conservation Society. Bronx, New York. July 1996.

BEFORE BRINGING YOUR GREY HOME

The decision to purchase an African grey should not be made lightly. Like dogs or cats, traditional domesticated pets, African greys are companion creatures. Therefore, you must not only decide whether a grey is right for you, but also whether you are right for a grey.

Are You a Grey Person?

✔ Why do you want a parrot? Are you interested in close companionship, or do you like to collect parrots?

✔ Will you stay committed, even when faced with major lifestyle changes, such as job loss or having a baby?

✔ African greys are dusty birds. Their feather dust can exacerbate allergies, asthma, and other bronchial problems. Do you have airborne allergies?

✔ Greys can be messy. Will you be calm if your grey poops on your rug, throws food on the walls, or damages furniture and wall paper?

✔ Greys pick up on our moods. They connect better with humans who are calm, grounded, and centered. Are you that type of person most of the time?

✔ Will you stay committed to your grey, even if it displays behavior disorders, such as screaming or feather picking?

✔ Will you invest time and money into veterinary care, proper nutrition, equipment, toys, and grooming services?

Are you a grey person?

✔ Are you prepared to work through the jealousy if your grey favors another family member?

What Is the Ideal Age to Buy?

Babies: The ideal time to buy a baby grey is between the ages of three- and five-months old. Purchase it after it has been weaned by the breeder or pet store. Weaning is the process by which a chick learns to eat on its own.

Some disreputable breeders/pet store personnel may try to convince you to wean it yourself. Although you may save money, you will pay in the long run because it is easy to kill a baby parrot while weaning it. Here are some examples of what can go wrong:

• **Right amount of formula?** Feeding too much or too little formula can cause many problems. Overfeeding can result in crop souring or bacterial growth. Underfeeding can result in nutritional problems.

• **Right temperature?** Formula that is too cold can cause a sour crop. Formula that is too hot can burn the crop.

• **Right thickness?** If the formula is too thick it can cause a sour crop or bacterial problems.

• **Right system?** Openings to the crop and air sac/lungs are located in the same area of the parrot's mouth. If the syringe is inserted into the air sac by mistake, the parrot may die from asphyxiation.

Older greys: There are many older greys that need new homes. They may range from the ages of 9 or 10 months to 40 years old. People impulsively purchase them. But once their interests change, or if there is a behavior difficulty, they discard the parrots. Another chapter in this book discusses strategies for rehabilitating them. If you have the commitment to work with an older rescue bird, the experience can be rewarding.

Preparing the Home

Choosing A Cage

African greys need large cages. However, cages that are at least three or four feet wide are more ideal than tall ones. This provides more space for them to "hang out" and play on the bottom of their cages. Furthermore, many grey owners prefer shorter cages so they can construct play-top areas on them. However, cage-top play areas should not be above eye level because it is more difficult to handle a parrot that is out of reach and playing above one's head. In choosing a cage, there are many options to investigate:

✔ Spacing between the bars should be no wider than one inch. Your grey should not be able to stick its head between the bars.

✔ Some cages have both horizontal and vertical bars. This provides more variety and ease of climbing.

✔ Some cages offer wide doors that swing open and act as a perch. Wide doors also make it easier for you to reach in the cage to clean.

✔ Many cages feature food bowl slots with locks or doors so that food can be inserted from outside the cage.

✔ Some cages feature aprons to prevent poop and food from falling on the floor. I do not recommend that you use them if your grey is clumsy. If you're concerned about a mess around the cage, purchase a plastic office mat from any business supply store to place under the cage.

Some aviculturists recommend removing the cage floor grate because many parrots injure themselves on them when they fall off their perches. If you can't remove it, place soft materials, such as a towel covered by newspaper, on top of the grate. This will soften the blow if your grey falls. However, some owners prefer not to remove the grates because they do not want their parrots to chew the paper in the bottom of the cage.

Although there are many product options for covering the cage floor, I believe the safest and cheapest alternative is black and white newsprint. Other alternatives, such as walnut shells and corn cobs, make it too easy to overlook poop and discarded food. This can result in bacterial and fungal growth that can make your bird sick. For example, corncob bedding can harbor Aspergillus spores that can lead to aspergillosis.

Once you've found the ideal cage, check it over carefully to make sure there are no sharp edges or wires sticking out. Make sure that the paint is not chipped or rusted. Cages with ornate designs may be dangerous because "climbing toes" may get caught in them.

Cage Accessories

✔ **Food bowls:** You will need at least three or four bowls for your Grey's cage:

1) for water;
2) dry foods;
3) wet foods, such as vegetables; and
4) one more for containing hand-held toys.

Most large cages offer slots for three bowls. You can purchase a fourth cup holder through your bird store. I recommend that you purchase the heavy crock bowls that playful greys can't tip over. Wet foods should be served only in stainless steel or ceramic bowls. Avoid using galvanized ones because this can lead to zinc toxicosis.

✔ **Perches:** Greys' feet can get tired from constantly standing on the same type of perch. Therefore, the objective is to provide perches that have a variety of widths, lengths, and types of materials. Greys feel more secure on perches that they can wrap their feet at least three quarters of the way around. Anything wider than one inch is usually too large. A variety of perch textures, such as wood and rope, should be provided. The rope perches and swings are particularly good for clumsy or handicapped greys. Check them daily and cut off any loose threads that may catch toes. It is recommended that you sand spots on slippery manzanita perches to improve the grip. Concrete perches are popular for gripping and keeping nails trimmed. But do not put more than one in the cage because they can irritate your bird's feet. Do not place sandpaper covers on the perches. Greys also like swings and rope boing toys.

✔ **Sleeping cages:** In the wild, greys fly long distances between their roosts and feeding places. So, they are instinctively used to sleeping in different areas from where they spend the day. Further, they need to have at least 10 to 12 hours of dark, uninterrupted sleep. As a result, if their day cages are in a noisy area, such as the family room, they need to sleep in a quieter place. I recommend that your parrot sleep in a separate cage from its day cage in a quiet room. Sleeping cages can be small, even as small as a traveling case. Since many greys experience night fright, I recommend that the sleeping cage be as sparse as possible. For example, remove toys so that the parrot doesn't get tangled in them during a fright. The sleeping cage only needs to contain a simple perch and water.

✔ **Cage covers:** I highly recommend the use of cage covers. Not only do they provide security, but they also protect your parrot from drafts. They can be as simple as a navy sheet. Wash them weekly because many greys preen in the middle of the night, and the feather dust collects on the sheet.

Real Estate: Location, Location

1. Cage layout: Your grey's cage is its home. Its perches, toys, and play areas should be placed to make it comfortable. For example, the perches should be placed at different levels so that your parrot can climb around the cage with ease. They should be far enough apart that your bird does not poop on one while perching on another. They should be spaced so that it can get to its food bowls. The toys should be positioned so that the shavings from chewing them don't fall into the food bowls. If you have a young, clumsy grey, place its perches and toys at lower levels in the cage until the bird is more coordinated. Set up the cage before your feathered companion comes home. However, make adjustments as you observe how your parrot maneuvers around it.

Above: Do not buy an unweaned baby.

Above right: Greys are wonderful companion creatures.

Below: Many greys like to play at the bottom of their cages.

Young greys have dark eyes and dark tips on their tails.

Many greys like to play on top of their cages.

2. Cage location: The following options should be considered:

✔ Greys are highly social flock animals. They prefer to be where the human action is. Therefore, they are happier in places, such as family rooms, where they can interact with their human flock members. This is a better alternative for a grey than being placed in a separate bird room, which is away from the human flock.

✔ Position the cage so that your parrot can monitor the activity in the room. The back of the cage should be against a wall for security. If there is more than one parrot, place them in different parts of the room so that they have their own territories.

✔ There must be good lighting; but make sure your parrot is not in direct sunlight. Keep it away from drafts from windows, heaters, air conditioners, and doors opening and closing.

✔ Watch your parrot's reactions to its location. Outgoing greys may prefer to be in busy areas. Shyer ones may prefer to be in quieter locations, so they can observe the action. Many greys enjoy being near windows where they can observe the backyard birds. However, if your grey's cage is near a window or sliding glass door, at least one side should be backed against a wall. This will help it feel more secure if there is a predatory attack on the outside animals. Some greys become nervous when hawks or airplanes fly overhead; therefore, placement under a skylight is not recommended. Observe your bird's reactions to objects and fixtures near its cage.

Other Accessories

✔ **Portable perches:** Play stands are a must!!! There are many interesting designs with ladders, swings, perches, and toys on them. One of the most important features is to have a perch that your grey cannot climb off.

✔ **Travel cages:** Travel cages are needed for emergencies, visits to the vet, and travel. Since I travel a lot with my "girls," Merlin Tewillager and Sweet Pea, we have many types of travel cages: basic plastic pet carriers with perches drilled in them; flat plastic carriers with a grill top for flying (airplane regulation size); and wire cages that are light but have enough room for a few perches, toys, and food.

✔ **Humidifiers:** Investigate humidifiers that use cold water, instead of steam. They are safer than steam humidifiers because they cultivate less bacterial growth. Avoid any that are coated with Teflon or other PTFE materials. Humidifiers should be cleaned regularly and kept at least six feet from the cage.

✔ **Air purifiers:** Greys are very dusty. Air purifiers improve breathing for both greys and their owners.

Full spectrum lighting: Birds have tetrachromatic vision, which means they see with four color channels: ultraviolet, blue, green and red. Therefore, to see properly, they need lighting that also provides ultraviolet light. Human vision, by contrast, does not process ultraviolet light. Therefore, color perceptions are very different between birds and humans.[1] Regular home electric incandescent lightbulbs and conventional neon lamps do not adequately provide ultraviolet light. Therefore, lighting sources that provide full-spectrum lighting for birds, such as Vitalites and OTT Lights, are highly recommended. Full-spectrum lighting also helps to activate the conversion of vitamin D3 for calcium absorption (see Teaching Your Grey to Eat a Balanced Diet).

Indoor/Outdoor Flight Aviaries

Some owners provide large twenty-foot flight cages for exercise. They can be erected either inside the house or outdoors. Many companies provide special cages, built to specification. If the aviaries are outdoors, they must be placed in an area of the yard that is safe from predators. The cages must be strong enough so that they cannot be bitten through, either by predators trying to get in or by parrots trying to chew out. They must be built above the ground so that vermin cannot burrow in. There should be shelter areas in them where the parrots can escape from heat, rain, and other inclement weather.

Greys become nervous about anything that is new. They are particularly wary about new cages that are unfamiliar and that look different from their regular cages. Therefore, introduce your companion slowly to the new aviary.

If you place your bird outdoors in a "regular" cage for fresh air and sunshine, do not leave it unattended. Greys panic when predators stalk them. They frantically flap around in the cage. A smart hawk can grab its prey through the bars and kill it in an instant. A friend's grey loved to play in a

Some Plants Considered Potentially Poisonous

American Yew *(Taxus canadensis)*
Azalea *(Rhododendron canadensis)*
Baneberry *(Actaea* species)
Bittersweet Nightshade *(Solanum dulcamara)*
Black Locust *(Robinia pseudoacacia)*
Bloodroot *(Sanguinario* species)
Buckthorn *(Rhamnus* species)
Buttercup *(Ranunculus* species)
Caladium *(Caladium* species)
Calla Lilly *(Zantedeschia aethiopica)*
Cherry Tree *(Prunus* species)
Christmas Candle *(Pedilanthus tithymaloides)*
Clematis *(Clematis* species)
Cowslip *(Caltha* species)
Daphne *(Daphne* species)
Dieffenbachia *(Dieffenbachia* species)
English Ivy *(Hedera helix)*
English Yew *(Taxus baccata)*
Laburnum *(Laburnum anagyroides)*
Hemlock *(Conium maculatum)*
Henbane *(Hyoscyamus niger)*
Honey Locust *(Gleditsia triacathos)*
Horse Chestnut *(Aesculus* species)

Hydrangea *(Hydrangea* species)
Indian Turnip *(Arisaema triphyllum)*
Iris *(Iris* species)
Jack-in-the-Pulpit *(Arisaema triphyllum)*
Jimsonweed *(Datura* species)
Larkspur *(Delphinium* species)
Locoweed *(Astragalus mollissimus)*
Lords and Ladies *(Arum* species)
May Apple *(Podophyllum* species)
Mistletoe *(Santalales* species)
Monkshood *(Aconitum* species)
Morning Glory *(Ipomoea* species)
Mountain Laurel *(Kalmia latifolia)*
Philodendron *(Philodendron* species)
Pokeweed *(Phytolacca amaricana)*
Rhubarb *(Rheum rhaponticum)*
Snowdrop *(Ornithogalum umbellatum)*
Tobacco *(Nicotiana* species)
Virginia Creeper *(Panthenocissus quinquefolia)*
Wisteria *(Wisteria* species)
Western Yew *(Taxus breviflora)*
    This list is not exhaustive. Carefully check every plant before allowing your parrot near it.

cage in the garage a few times per week. One day it was killed by a raccoon that reached in the cage when the parrot was left unattended.

Household Dangers

   Due to their small size, high metabolic rate, low body fat, and efficient respiratory system, birds can die quickly when exposed to airborne toxins.

✔ **Nonstick cookware:** One of the worst dangers is the nonstick ingredient, polytetrafluoroethylene (PTFE), which comes under many brand names, such as Teflon, Supra, and Silverstone. When cookware with PTFE (any nonstick cookware) is overheated, it breaks down and emits several types of organic gases and hydrofluoric acid. The gases and acid attack the parrots' air sacs almost immediately. Once nonstick surfaces are scratched or tainted in any way, they are susceptible to breakdown of the acid

Do not allow your grey to chew any leaves or branches until you know they are safe.

Congo chicks can be endearing.

Introductions to other family pets must be closely supervised.

or gases at regular cooking temperatures. This can be deadly to your grey. Read labels and avoid all products with nonstick coatings: pots/pans, space heaters, irons, hair dryers, heat lamps, ironing board covers, drip pans, griddles, woks, electric skillets, coffee makers, pizza pans, and many others.

✔ **Avoid the following products:** carpet fresheners, scented candles, heavy cleaning chemicals, perfumes, self-cleaning ovens, plug-in air fresheners, and aerosol sprays.

✔ **Secondhand cigarette smoke can be lethal to your parrot.** Nicotine passed from your hands or lips can enter your parrot's

Portable play stands give greys more playing opportunities.

Greys love to destroy their toys.

Curious greys explore with their beaks.

system through its feet. If you smoke, quit! If you can't, smoke in a different room. Wash your hands and lips before handling your bird.

✔ **Avoid all products containing lead, zinc, and cadmium,** such as brass key rings, pennies, costume jewelry; artist paints and pencils, and so on. A friend's cockatoo almost died from zinc poisoning, which she concocted by mouthing a chain around her owner's neck. Some bird-related products also contain lead and zinc (see Teaching Your Grey Everyday Living Skills). They should be avoided.

Family Introductions

The Kids

Greys and kids get along. However, all contact must be closely supervised. Raucous behavior and teasing terrifies parrots. Kids should be taught to be calm; not to run around the cage; and not to hit or touch the cage bars. Give your children daily responsibilities for bird chores.

Other Pets

Like kids, contact with other pets should be supervised. Physical contact with other pets can be dangerous. A nip from an excited dog can harm your parrot. Even more caution is advised for contact with cats. They have bacteria in their teeth and claws that can kill parrots within hours, if not treated. It may be easier to train a kitten to respect a parrot. The nature of their relationship will depend on the confidence levels of your bird and the way in which you introduce the whole flock. Do not be surprised if, once your grey becomes comfortable

in your home, it manipulates the other pets, "Fido, bad dog . . . Go outside!"

Other Birds

Avian behavior consultant Sally Blanchard believes that birds already at home should be introduced to the new arrival slowly, even before it arrives. She recommends that the new bird's cage be set up with accessories. Pretend the new parrot is already there. When you are feeding the current flock, fiddle with the new cage.

Sometimes the arrival of a new bird can cause jealousy, particularly if you are closely bonded to another parrot. I found that by giving my first bonded bird the attention first, it became easier for it to accept when my attention went to the new bird.

If your parrot is your first bird, congratulations. A single parrot household can be very rewarding. Your grey needs lots of love and companionship when you are home.

As stated in Understanding the Nature of African Greys, some greys may have difficulties getting along with other parrots in your home. Closely supervise all introductions and interactions.

The quarantine: Germs travel, not only by contact, but also by air. Separate a new parrot from the other birds for a period to protect your current flock and the new arrival. The length of time may vary by circumstance, but a period of at least 45 days should give you enough time to watch your new grey and to receive the avian health results from your veterinarian. The "new bird" health check-up should be conducted by a qualified vet before you bring it home (day of purchase).

A quarantine entails wearing separate clothes, including shoes, when you spend time in each bird room. Clean each room with different materials. Prepare, feed, and clean up utensils and equipment separately. This may seem complicated, but when it comes to the health of your loved ones, it's worth it. Request your avian veterinarian to recommend quarantine procedures, based on your individual circumstances.

The Purchase Decision

Choosing the Right Breeder

Socialized babies have the best start at being happy, secure adults. Interview and compare the breeders and stores thoroughly. Here are some questions to ask.

✔ Do they seem to care about the birds and what their new owners are like?

✔ Do they allow the babies to briefly learn to fly at fledging, before clipping their wings?

✔ How do they feed the babies? What kind of foods do they wean the babies on?

✔ At what age are their babies weaned?

✔ How many do they wean at a time?

✔ What type of socializing practices do they use?

✔ How do they play with the babies? (Observe them with the babies.)

✔ What kind of questions do they ask you?

Observing the Chick

Look closely at the chick's appearance.

✔ Does it seem alert?

✔ Are its nostrils and eyes clear?

✔ Is its vent area clear?

✔ Do the feathers look shiny and healthy?

✔ Are its feet clean and healthy looking?

✔ Does it appear socialized?

✔ Will it climb on your finger or hand when you stick it out?

✔ What is its personality like?

✔ How does it react to you?

The Final Decision

Let the chick choose you. If you feel a heart connection, it is right for you. If you don't feel a connection, keep looking until you do.

[1]Ruediger, T. Korbel, Ulrike Gropp, D.V.M. "Ultraviolet Perceptions in Birds," Association of Avian Veterinarians, 1999 Proceedings.

GETTING TO KNOW YOUR GREY

It is normal to feel nervous during the first few days of your new parrot's arrival. Your companion is anxious too. Relax and focus on helping it feel comfortable. The moment you bring it home, place your new companion on your hand or on its carrier, wherever it is more comfortable.

Surviving the First Few Days

Calmly tell your parrot how happy you are to have it there. Give it time to adjust to its new surroundings. Then introduce it to the room. Walk around the room while holding your bird. Show it areas of the room. Talk about and touch different parts of the cage. Be exuberant and excited. If your new companion doesn't appear frightened by the cage, place it on top. Let it climb around to explore. Once your bird appears comfortable, place it in the cage. Encourage it to explore inside. Provide it food and talk with it reassuringly. Then give it time to rest and adjust.

Spend lots of time over the first few weeks handling and reassuring the parrot. However, it also needs time alone to adjust to its new home. The appropriate mix of handling and alone time will depend on its personality and how well it was previously socialized.

Relax and make your new companion comfortable.

Setting Routines

The more involved your companion is in your family activities, the happier it will be. At a minimum, it will require two to three hours of out-of-the-cage time everyday. This should include at least fifteen to thirty minutes of daily concentrated time focused only on your parrot, without competition from the television, telephone, or computer. Many grey owners have special games they play with their birds during this period. My Sweet Pea and I play a game of soccer. We bat a wooden ball back and forth, between beak and hand.

We all have daily routines. When we get up in the morning, we follow the same steps everyday to get dressed and go to work. Greys are no different. They also prefer daily routines. But it is not a good idea to keep them on the same rigid daily schedules. As behavior consultant Sally Blanchard says, if you keep feeding your grey at six o'clock every night, seldom veering from the schedule to five-thirty or six-thirty, it will manipulate you to stick to

TIP

Do's and Don'ts

Remember that your new companion has just separated from its pet store or breeder flock. It is completely on its own for the first time. If it is an older bird coming from another home, it may be lonely and confused. Therefore, for the first few days, conduct errands over short periods. For example, go to the bank and return. Then go to the grocery store and return. Always tell the bird "I'll be back," so that your parrot becomes reassured that you will return. It may help to bring your new parrot home over a weekend, so that you will not be separated from it for very long periods during the first few days.

Your new companion is adjusting to many things in the first few days and weeks, which can be stressful. Therefore, restrict the introductions to the "family flock." Bring in your friends at a later time. Some "don'ts."

✔ Do not introduce other animal family members until your parrot has adjusted.
✔ Do not introduce it to the rest of the house until it is comfortable with its current surroundings.
✔ Do not introduce it physically to other bird family members until all veterinary test results are in and the "new bird quarantine" period has passed.

the timetable. However, do not feed your parrot at nine o'clock in the evening. This can result in a cranky and hungry bird. Keep a flexible schedule within reason. Change it often. The more you can mix up the daily schedule, the less "set in its ways" your grey will become.

One of the most dangerous myths is that "greys can't tolerate change from a routine." This is *not* true. It is important to change their routines and introduce them to new experiences. But it must be done at their own pace. Everyone gets nervous the first few times they try something. African grey breeder Pamela Clark suggests introducing your grey to change in "increments." For example, I introduced my Merlin Tewillager to travel by following a step-by-step process from one experience to the next. We did not move to the next step until she was comfortable with the previous one. First, I made sure she was comfortable with visitors in our home. Then I introduced her to strangers in our New York City apartment lobby. Then we graduated to brief visits at friends' homes, and so on.

The more experiences your grey is exposed to at its own pace, the more relaxed it will become. In contrast, the less exposure it receives, the more nervous, myopic, and fearful it can become.

Dealing with Fears

There is a difference between a fearful grey and a reticent one that is nervous and squawks to protest something new in its routine. A truly fearful grey will show many of the fear behaviors discussed in HOW-TO: Read Body Language at the end of this chapter. This is a sign that you need to back up and work with it more slowly.

Observe the situations and experiences that make your grey afraid. The more you can contain a fear and reassure your parrot that everything is okay, the more quickly it will overcome the fear. For example, both of my greys were afraid of shadows on the wall. Therefore, I made a shadow of my hand on the living room wall. I said "shadow," while laughing and making patterns with my hands. I repeated this activity for weeks, until they were relaxed. Then I brought each bird to the wall to beak its own shadow. When they tapped their beaks against the wall, I laughed and said "shadow." Now, whenever they are nervous from a sudden shadow, I say "shadow." They immediately relax. A friend Ellen Zadalis helped her grey Jocko overcome his fear of bumps in the road by yelling "Wheeee!" every time they rode over one. After a while, he began saying "wheee!" himself.

As mentioned in chapter one, it is the instinct of your new grey companion to react quickly to anything sudden or new in your home. Its power of observation is so strong that it will notice every minute detail, such as a box that has been moved from its place. It may be afraid of anything new that you bring into the room. Always place a new object below your waist and on the side of you that is furthest from the cage when you bring it into the room. This will help your parrot feel more secure.

Clumsiness and How to Help It

In the wild a young parrot must learn to fly and land before becoming food independent. It needs confidence and flying skills to follow its parents to learn what to eat. This is called fledging. Many breeders replicate this process by allowing a ten-day to two-week period for the grey babies to learn to fly before being clipped. They transform from being wobbly, unsure babies to confident, coordinated young chicks. Grey chicks that are not allowed to fledge can become clumsy for the first few years of their lives.

Clumsy parrots can suffer serious injuries, such as broken bones and split keels (the skin over the breast bone tears open). If they continue to hurt themselves, they may become insecure and possibly turn phobic. Therefore, take precautions if your parrot is clumsy.

✔ Always check with your veterinarian first to make sure there are no physical problems causing the clumsiness.

✔ Take out the grate and pad the cage bottom with soft materials under the newsprint, such as towels. If the grate doesn't come out, place towels and newsprint on top of it. Also, pad the floor around the cage and playpen with soft materials, such as towels and rugs.

✔ Position cage perches so they are not on top of each other. Do not overload the cage with toys. If your parrot becomes frightened or flutters to get its balance, it may get hurt by falling on other perches or getting tangled in the toys.

✔ At night, place your grey in a small sleeping cage that has only the sleeping perch and a food bowl with water. If it roosts (sleeps) in its day cage, make sure all perches, toys, and food bowls are removed from any areas where your companion may fall if it loses its balance in its sleep.

Proper Nail and Wing Clipping

If your grey's nails and wings are clipped too short, it can become clumsy. On top of that, a hard fall or two can make the parrot nervous and insecure. Some greys have become so insecure that they turned phobic of their owners who chased after them to comfort them after a fall (refer to Teaching Your Grey Everyday Living Skills).

The overall objective of a wing clip is to cut the wings short enough so that the parrot cannot fly a long distance. However, the wings must be long enough to allow the parrot to land without hurting itself if it falls. It should be able to fly a short distance, no higher than a few feet off the ground; but it should not be able to get a lift. Here are some basic pointers:

✔ Never clip only one wing. This results in an imbalance and severe loss of control.

Greys like to have their heads rubbed by their new owners.

✔ Do not leave the end primary flight feathers intact. It is too easy for them to get caught in the cage bars.

✔ Do not clip blood feathers. They are easily identified in blood-filled sheaths that look dark red.

✔ Clip as few primary feathers as possible. Start by clipping four or five. However, if your parrot can fly a long distance, clip one or two more from each wing.

✔ Never assume that a clipped bird cannot fly outside. Even a parrot with a short clip can fly, with the right breeze, or if a sudden sound or movement frightens it.

✔ Long nails enable parrots to grip onto perches. You only need to dull the sharp tips by filing them.

Greys are affectionate in their own way.

✔ If you do not have experience clipping wings and nails, take your bird to an experienced veterinarian or avian practitioner. Make sure they do not clip too short.

Cuddling

Generally, African greys are not cuddly like cockatoos. However, they are affectionate in their own way. In the wild, chicks have the physical comfort of their parents and clutch mates. In captivity, most well-socialized babies will want to be cuddled by their owners. However, as they mature, they can become less interested in being cuddled. Perhaps this relates to the instinctive need to physically interact only with a mate.

Even then, it is important to maintain a physical connection with your grey. The best time to work with it is when it is feeling sleepy, either before bedtime, early in the morning, or during mid-afternoon before naptime. Start with a few gentle head or beak rubs. Then slowly move to other parts of the body. Let your grey tell you what it will/will not accept.

Developmental Stages

Like many other parrots, African greys learn in distinct developmental stages. There are certain windows of opportunity when some characteristics need to be developed at early stages. Therefore, greys that are carefully nurtured by

The first six weeks is a time of sleeping and eating.

breeders, pet stores, and previous owners will have an easier transition into your home. Although it is not possible to replicate experiences from the wild, they should be given opportunities that stimulate curiosity and provide challenges to help them grow in self-confidence.

The First Six Weeks

Both Timneh and Congo greys lay an average of three-to-five eggs at two-or-three day intervals. The incubation period lasts generally one month. The first six weeks is primarily a time of physical growth: eating and sleeping. Depending on the philosophy of the breeder, the chicks are taken from their parents' nest box at either two, four, or six weeks of age. Many breeders believe that the longer the chick remains with its parents, the more stable it will become.

Six-to-Nine Weeks

Grey breeder and behavior consultant Pamela Clark calls this period the "curiosity stage."[1] They become interested in actively exploring things around them. At approximately six weeks, her grey babies are placed in a cardboard box in the bottom compartment of a three stack cage. This provides the continuity and security of a cardboard box, but yet it gives them more space in which to explore food and toys. As they become more curious, they are allowed to explore other foods, toys, and humans on the floor of her home. Once they appear to have mastered this stage, they are graduated to the second level of the stack cage. It has a climbing and play area, where they face more challenges and so on. Her philosophy is to provide the babies "graduated challenges" that

build their self-confidence. This is similar to how parents teach their chicks.

Both breeders Phoebe Linden and Pamela Clark believe baby chicks must develop curiosity in this period. Breeders should provide many opportunities to foster curiosity, such as colorful toys, food, and space to physically explore.

Nine-to-Sixteen Weeks

This is the stage when the bird transforms from the awkward baby to the confident fledgling. Learning to fly is its *rite of passage* to independence. As discussed in the clumsiness section, many breeders allow a ten-day to two-week period of flying, before clipping their wings.

Wild chicks are dependent on their parents for food. From the moment they are born, their crops are filled before they're hungry. That's because crying and begging can attract predators. They are fed regurgitated foods. As they develop, they are also fed bits of regular food, in addition to the regurgitated food. Weaning begins once the chick is fledged. It is a gradual process where the chick continues to be fed regurgitated food, while learning to eat on its own. It is never forced to go hungry.

Phoebe Linden's "abundance weaning"[2] process replicates this *plentiful feeding* concept. Ms. Linden's baby parrots are fed as much as they can comfortably handle. They are never allowed to go hungry. Similar to the wild parrots that allow the babies to nibble on and play with bits of regular food in the nest, Ms. Linden provides bowls of fruits and vegetables to pin-feathered chicks, long before they are ready to eat them. Overtime, they begin to play with and eventually nibble on them, in addition to their formula. These are called "transition

Break open pin feathers by gently pinching the very tip (see HOW-TO: Read Body Language).

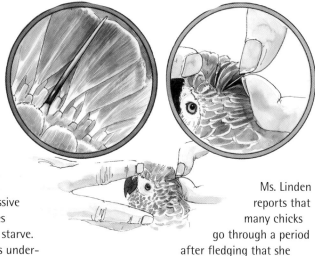

foods." Ms. Linden believes this experience is a critical part of learning adult eating skills.

In the wild, being *plentifully fed* provides psychological security and well-being. In contrast, when food is scarce, the strongest, most aggressive nestlings and fledglings are the ones who get the food. The weaker ones starve. Therefore, hunger means death. It is understandable that many captive-bred babies become insecure when their breeders force them to wean too early by denying them food. It triggers an instinctive fear of death.

Food Independent to Twelve Months

In the wild at this stage, it is suspected that young Congos remain in their family units. They are supervised by their parents and possibly older greys from previous clutches that are not currently raising young. Also, it is theorized that the Timnehs leave their family units to join other juveniles within the flock.

In captivity, this age is when the baby grey joins its new home. It is a crucial time for the new owner to carry forward parenting instruction to help the baby adjust to its environment. It is a time of building security and behavior patterns. Activities, such as bathing, that have been established by the breeder/pet store should be continued. New toys, assorted foods, and new experiences should be introduced at the baby's pace.

Ms. Linden reports that many chicks go through a period after fledging that she describes as the "lost in the woods" stage. In the wild, the new fledgling that is learning to explore and forage on its own also faces the fear of being lost and left behind. She says, "a baby who feels lost in the woods may do these things: call repetitively and plaintively, pace or weave back and forth as if they were going to jump from their perch, jump down from the perch, seem unsettled, nervous, and crave attention."[3] At this stage, chicks that exhibit these behaviors need reassurance. Ms. Linden advises new owners to comfort them and not to worry about "spoiling" them.

Both baby and adult greys tend to eat less when introduced to new situations, such as coming into a new home. If your new companion appears to be crying and begging often with its wings lowered, it may be hungry. Again, the weaning process in the wild is gradual, and a fledgling continues to be fed as it develops its eating skills. Even if your grey has been weaned or if it's an older grey, spoonfeed it warm, pureed foods in addition to its regular foods.

Twelve Months to Three Years

In the wild, Congo juveniles leave their families and join groups of other juveniles. Similar to human teenagers, they are more influenced by their peers than parents. It is an important period for building self-confidence, learning to communicate, and getting along with each other. They are influenced hormonally to begin seeking suitable mates.

In the home, this may translate to a grey that suddenly drops its favored human for another member of the household. As stated in chapter one, if this happens, do not take it personally.

Phoebe Linden describes this period as one when young parrots move through the compliant juvenile and more turbulent adolescent stages. She says, "During adolescence, we see challenges within daily interaction: the adolescent ignores established rules, tests limits, and tries to shift power in the flock . . . The adolescent experience reflects early development and predicts adult behavior."[4] However, a stormy adolescent period does not have to transpire, if the caretaker carefully reads body language and socializes the parrot.

Three Years and Older

By three years old, greys have begun to reach adulthood. Their true personalities are established. Although they don't become sexually mature until five or six years old, they may have begun exhibiting sexual advances at the preferred mate (refer to HOW-TO: Read Body Language). Even though it is an honor to be loved, it is best to let the parrot know that you appreciate its affections; but do not initiate any physical activity, such as hugging or touching parts of its back, during this time.

As the young parrot matures, it views its favored human and members of the household

Baby chicks need toys, food, and space to explore.

"Transition foods" help baby greys develop healthy adult eating skills.

as flock members to be respected at its level. I conducted an informal survey of *Grey Play Round Table* magazine subscribers who owned older greys (nine years and older). I found that the greys that were continually socialized became more confident, calmer and more relaxed as they aged. However, those that were confined to their homes without the introduction of new challenges and experiences became more nervous than their earlier years. Therefore, it is important to continue the socialization process throughout the African grey's life.

[1]Clark, Pamela. "Minus 29 Days and Counting," *Grey Play Round Table*. Tewillager Publishing, division of Equatorial Group, LTD; Old Chatham, New York. Summer 1999, p. 5.

[2]Linden, Phoebe. *Abundantly Avian: The Compiled Works of Phoebe Linden from the Pet Bird Report*. Santa Barbara Bird Farm, Santa Barbara, California, 1999, pp. 43–46.

[3]Linden, Phoebe. *Abundantly Avian: The Compiled Works of Phoebe Linden from the Pet Bird Report*. Santa Barbara Bird Farm, Santa Barbara, California, 1999, p. 10.

[4]Linden, Phoebe. *Abundantly Avian: The Compiled Works of Phoebe Linden from the Pet Bird Report*. Santa Barbara Bird Farm, Santa Barbara, California, 1999, pp. 121, 125.

HOW-TO: READ BODY

The best way to get to know your new companion is to observe it. Notice how it explores its cage. Watch its body language. Be alert to its reactions.

Signs of Relaxation

✔ **Beak Grinding:** Beak grinding is the sound of a very contented bird. The parrot vibrates its lower mandible (beak) and tongue against the upper mandible. This results in a soft, grinding noise. Parrots usually grind their beaks just before drifting off to sleep.

✔ **Fluffing:** When a grey is very relaxed, it often fluffs out or loosens its feathers, particularly around the head and neck. This can also be a sign of potential sickness. Therefore, if your bird remains fluffed for a long period of time and it is abnormally quiet, contact your avian veterinarian.

✔ **Head in Wing:** Most often greys sleep at night with their heads tucked under their wings. They can often be seen resting in that fashion during the day, particularly while their owners are away at work.

✔ **Preening:** Greys have over 2,000 feathers on their bodies. They spend a lot of time cleaning them by placing each feather in the beak and sweeping the tongue along the feather. They also rub their heads against a preen gland at the base of the tail that emits an oil that is then rubbed on their feathers. Although preening is instinctive, it also is a learned skill. Some young chicks, without the benefit of watching older parrots preen properly, may either preen too little and look a little scruffy, or be overzealous and overpreen. If your new grey companion seems to have a problem, let it watch an older grey preen. If your grey wants its head to be preened, it will fluff out its feathers and lower its head.

Parrots also preen to care for new feathers. These new feathers, called "pin feathers," initially come out in a hard sheath called a quill that protects them while they are developing. A parrot in a heavy molt can be cranky because the prickly pin feathers are sensitive. Molting causes a physical drain on the body.

Tip: Your grey may elicit your help in breaking open the quill sheaths on its head when the feathers are ready. Preening a pin feather too early can result in pain. Wait until it feels less stiff, or moves about more flexibly, and the tip of the sheath has a whitish look. Gently prick the whitish part, or the very tip of the sheath, between your fingernails. The whitish material will begin to come off. Then go to the next pin feather. The purpose of pricking the tip of the pin feather is to start the process of opening. You do not need to prick all the way down. The sheath will come off naturally over time.

✔ **Vibrating Chest:** Do not be alarmed when your grey's chest feathers quiver. This is not a sign of nervousness. Greys' feathers move when they are feeling emotion. When *only* the chest feathers are vibrating, it is usually a sign of happiness.

✔ **Standing on One Foot:** A relaxed grey usually stands on one foot, with the other tucked under its breast.

Signs of Fear

✔ **Freezing:** In the wild, predators identify their prey by movement. Therefore, prey animals freeze to avoid being noticed. If your grey suddenly freezes, it is instinctively reacting to a sudden

LANGUAGE

movement or noise, or it senses that something is wrong.

✔ **Flattened Feathers:** When greys relax, they fluff out their feathers. When they are afraid, they flatten their feathers.

✔ **Growling:** An African grey sometimes growls when it is frightened of something in its territory.

✔ **Whole Body Shaking:** In contrast to the chest quivering alone, a grey with a trembling body is usually afraid of something. It may also be breathing deeply with wide, staring eyes.

Signs of Anger

✔ **Feathers Standing Up on Body:** When a grey is protecting its territory or is in attack mode, it puffs out its feathers to look larger than it is. This is usually a warning that it will bite, if provoked.

✔ **Eyes Pinning:** When your grey puffs out its feathers and narrows its pupils into slits, called pinning, it is usually preparing to bite. However, if your parrot's body is relaxed and it is pinning its eyes, this usually is a sign that it is concentrating on something, such as listening to you.

Signs of Love/Courtship

✔ **Regurgitation:** In the wild, birds regurgitate food to feed either their young or a mate. If your grey starts bobbing its head, pinning its eyes and regurgitates a liquidlike substance, consider this a great compliment. It is trying to feed you. Even if it seems disgusting, take the substance in your hand and thank your bird. However, if your parrot regurgitates for a long period of time and it shows other signs of illness, contact your avian veterinarian immediately.

✔ **Groaning:** If your grey lowers its wings, quivers, and groans, it is feeling love toward you. It is better to let it know that you love it, but do not respond physically until it has calmed down.

Signs of Nervousness

✔ **Nail Biting/Wing Flapping:** Greys are known for chewing their nails. This should not be a concern. However, a popular nervous grey habit is to incessantly chew its nails on a foot and then flap its wings frantically. Sometimes it is also a sign that the bird is hungry or tired.

✔ **Hyperactivity:** Some nervous greys appear to act hyperactive when nervous, tired, or overly hungry.

Other Body Language Signs

✔ **Yawning/Head Shaking:** If you notice your grey yawning or shaking its head, it may be dislodging a feather that is stuck in its ear. It may have something, such as a seed, stuck in its esophagus. Or it may truly be yawning. Birds are sensitive to sounds and vibrations that humans are not aware of; therefore, constant head shaking could also be a reaction to something in your environment, such as a loud noise or low vibrating machine. Do not be overly concerned with these activities, unless they persist and you see signs of illness.

✔ **Sneezing:** Greys sneeze or sometimes stick their claws in their nostrils (nares) to dislodge particles, such as feather dust. This should not be a concern. However, if you notice a discharge from the nostrils, contact your avian veterinarian. If your grey coughs *like a human*, don't worry. It is only an imitation. The human cough is one of the most popular sounds that greys like to mimic.

TEACHING YOUR GREY EVERYDAY LIVING SKILLS

Survival of baby chicks in the wild depends on how well they are taught by their parents. The parents teach the chicks how and what to eat, how to fly and land, how to preen, how to recognize and avoid predators, how to relate to other flock members, and many other skills.

Once the chicks have fledged, their parents encourage them to explore independently. They maintain supervision through contact calls.

The parents teach by guidance and demonstration. For example, they fly from branch to branch and call the chicks to follow. They teach their babies to forage by doing it first. The chicks experience a learning process similar to human children. The first reaction to a challenge may be fear and anticipation. But after constant encouragement by the parents, the first attempt is made. After several attempts and finally success, the "Yahoo-I-did-it" exhilaration comes and self-confidence builds.

Four basic principles must always be followed when teaching your new grey companion:

1. The more fun you are having, the more intrigued your companion will become about the activity. Act like a child.

2. Take one step at a time, and in increments. If your grey becomes nervous, go back to the last step until it becomes comfortable.

Teach your grey in small steps, one increment at a time.

3. Keep experimenting with different angles until one works. Be patient. Do not give up after trying something only a few times.

4. Make sure your grey feels safe and secure with each step.

Forms of Teaching

Demonstration

My friend Nancy Sheffer teaches her greys to play with toys by playing with them herself. She fiddles with them, day after day, until her parrots become curious about them. She sits on the floor, giggling. She shows them how to play with the toys. This form of demonstration teaching extends into all aspects of daily activities, such as trying new foods and introducing showers.

Tip: Greys want objects that their owners constantly use but keep away from them, such as ink pens and pencils. The more possessive you act about a new toy, the more curious your parrot will become.

Coaching

I remember watching my friend Eva Huebner encourage her grey Domino to explore areas in their living room on his own. She was always there in the background, similar to the wild parent encouraging its chick from a nearby branch. Domino knew she was there, if he needed her. Create games or challenges in your home that encourage exploration and independence. Get so excited about your African grey's accomplishments that it may think you won the lottery.

Exploration should be done in increments. It is best to encourage exploration in an area where your parrot feels safe, such as the living room. Exploration of new areas should be done together, with you and your chick as a flock group.

Modeling

Through her ground-breaking research and the development of the model/rival technique (M/R), Dr. Irene Pepperberg proved the success of teaching African greys through modeling behavior. The M/R technique contains three elements: social interaction, reference, and functionality. Two humans, a trainer and model, teach the parrots by replicating how they learn in the wild. They observe vocal exchanges between flock members (social interaction). The trainer asks the model "How many red four-corners (squares)?" If the model gives the right answer, he is rewarded with the object in question. He is allowed to manipulate and play with it. By observing the social interaction between the humans, the parrots learn that words have a direct correlation to a three-dimensional object (reference). They can obtain that object by using the correct words (functionality).

In addition to talking, variations of this modeling technique can be used to teach many living skills, such as eating nutritious foods, taking a shower, and playing games. Although the absence of the second person (the model) would prohibit exposure to interchange and role switching, variations of the technique also can be used in one-person households.

Sometimes other parrots can be used for modeling behavior. For example, through the *Grey Play Round Table* magazine, we have organized social groups that we call "Round Table groups." A small group of magazine subscribers and their African greys get together to socialize and share information. There have been instances where some nervous greys have become more relaxed from observing how other greys and their caretakers interact. There has been a noticeable difference in their behavior after attending the Round Table events. The gatherings are small. Each group has a strict health rule in place to ensure the safety of the parrots. They meet often, which allows the parrots and their caretakers to bond as cohesive flock groups.

Teaching to Talk

Generally, Congo African greys begin talking between 12 and 18 months old. Many say their first words or phrases much earlier, possibly before six months of age. However, the real chattering and speaking appropriately starts at a year or later. Timneh greys, by contrast, begin to chatter appropriately before one year of age. As stated in Understanding the Nature of African Grey Parrots, this does not mean that Timnehs are better talkers. It is believed they learn to talk earlier because they mature quicker. Once the Congos catch up, both sub-species are talented talkers.

✔ The moment you bring your new companion home, start talking to it. Talk about everything you're doing. But don't repeat the same word over and over (such as "Hello. . . hello."). This can be boring.

✔ Explain everything in a conversationlike tempo, as if talking with a child. However, do not use baby talk, unless you want it repeated later.

✔ Teach by association. Use the same phrases for the same tasks.

✔ Teach your grey companion to request things, such as "Want cheese," "Want window perch," or "Want big perch." By teaching your parrot to request objects and to be taken places, you are giving it a sense of control and power over its environment. Every time it requests something, give the object to the bird. In the beginning, it may request the object incessantly to watch you scramble. But over time, it will request only when it wants the object or action.

✔ Greys are social creatures that learn to talk more easily in interactive situations. They tend to tune out videos and recordings that are played either too often or for longer than fifteen minutes at a time. If you use recordings, interact with your parrot and the recording. Reinforce the words you're teaching by repeating them.

✔ In the beginning, do not push your companion to learn too many phrases at once. Use the early development stage to work on the parrot's enunciation and tonality. The incessant talking and chattering will come in time.

Some greys tend to speak more cognitively than others. It is theorized that greys that are housed in places, such as the family room, where they are exposed to human interaction tend to speak more cognitively than those that are housed separately from their caretakers, such as in bird rooms. The ones located away from human interaction (such as in bird rooms) do not have the exposure to learn the human flock language. Therefore, they tend to mimic phrases and use them as contact calls. Further, some greys learn to communicate their needs through other means, such as body language and specific chirps, and they rarely use human speech.

African greys love to mimic sounds, such as garbage trucks backing up, doorbells and telephones ringing, microwave and alarm beeps, garbage disposals, squeaky doors, hammering, burps, coughs, dripping water, the passing of gas, and barking dogs, to name a few. They will pick up on a sound that either interests or frightens them.

Teaching to Play

Many greys, particularly juveniles, are known to play hard with their toys. Many aviculturists believe the toys serve as surrogate flock mates. The parrots appear to turn them into imaginary friends and competitors. They attack, chew and then give them head rubs. They prefer toys they can destroy, such as wood, cardboard, rawhide and paper. They love to chew, shred, untie knots, and take things apart. Sometimes they are having such a good time that they forget to hold onto the perch and fall.

Greys are attracted to many types of toys, such as hanging chew toys, hand toys, homemade toys, and acrylic toys they bat around but can't destroy. They also like the companionship of mirror toys and the sound of copper bells. They like puzzler types of toys where they must chew a box or move a lever to get a nut.

Some greys like to play with baby toys.

Some greys prefer interactive toys, such as Playskool music boxes and farm animal sounds. African grey Twia Kasuku Sheffer is so taken with his music box that he awakens the household with it every morning. He taps a button with his beak, bounces up and down, clicking to the beat of "Old MacDonald Had a Farm." Then he taps it again for another children's song. He keeps himself amused for hours. He listens and bops to the music. Another grey,

Greys like to play with balls.

Morgan Levine, talks to her Furbie doll every day. Some greys like to cuddle with little stuffed animals.

Toys are mandatory for every grey household. Not only do they provide entertainment and companionship, but they also encourage the parrots to exercise and release pent-up energy. Most aviculturists recommend an average of three to five toys per cage, depending on the size of the cage. They should be rotated every few weeks to keep the parrots entertained.

Safety First

Observe the personality of your grey and use common sense in choosing a toy. For example, is your grey more aggressive with its toys? Does it prefer to chew chunks of wood? Or is it attracted to more delicate toys?

Purchase appropriately sized toys. Attach them to the cage securely. If the toy is attached by rope or leather, check it daily to avoid frays, snags or worn out places. In their book, *A Practical Guide to Parrot Toys and Play Areas*, Carol D'Arezzo and Lauren Shannon-Nunn recommend the use of untanned or vegetable tanned leather. They say that conventional leather contains uric acid and formaldehyde; therefore, items, such as leather shoelaces, should be avoided.[1]

The toy fastener must also be closely inspected. When purchasing chains, quick links, or any other fasteners, make sure they are stainless steel. Many are coated with zinc, which can be deadly to your parrot, particularly if it enjoys mouthing them. There are a number of other items that may contain zinc: galvanized wire cages, some galvanized food dishes, some formulations of powder coating on cages, and some toy parts. Zinc is an important nutrient when ingested as food; but it can be dangerous, when consumed from environmental sources. Here are some tips for keeping your grey safe.

✔ Inspect all new toys to make sure they won't catch your parrot's beak or toes. Holes or open spaces in toys must be smaller than your bird's head.

✔ Be wary of toys with long strands that can get frayed and catch beaks and toes. Keep them trimmed.

✔ Make sure that stuffed animal toys contain cotton or fabric stuffing, not tiny beads.

✔ Keep toys that may be questionable out of the cage. Save them for playtime on a playstand in your presence. For example, my grey Sweet Pea loves to chew rope, which can get frayed easily. Therefore, I save her rope swings for activities on her playstand, which I supervise.

Introducing New Toys

Your parrot will probably be nervous when it sees a new toy. Therefore, introduce it slowly.

✔ Leave it on the floor at the other end of the room from the cage. Move it a little closer every few days. At times, play with it with. Then put it back.

✔ Once it is on the floor beside the cage and your bird does not appear nervous, hang it on the outside of the cage. Always remove it from the cage, when you put your grey inside the cage.

✔ Move the toy inside, once your parrot appears relaxed and plays with it on top of the cage. However, your parrot may get nervous for the first few hours or days, after it has been placed in the cage. Therefore, always supervise your parrot and the new toy in the cage for the first few hours. If it appears nervous, put the

Rope toys that are frayed must be trimmed.

CHECKLIST

Toy Box Essentials

✔ Wooden beads from old toys (make sure not too small to be swallowed)

✔ Cardboard rolls (unscented rolls)

✔ Wooden shapes from the house, such as thread spools and clothes pins (no wires)

✔ Tinker toys

✔ Small cardboard boxes

✔ Envelopes and junk mail

✔ Popsicle and other wooden sticks

✔ Paper cups (avoid cups that are waxed)

✔ Plastic pen caps

toy back in its place. If you're not going to be available to supervise, remove the toy from the cage until you have time to be there.

Old Toys: What to Do?

Toys are expensive; therefore, reinvent them. Many greys love toy boxes. They can make their own decisions about which parts and textures to chew. Take parts of old toys that are safe and place them in a toy box. The toy box can be made either of wood or cardboard, such as an old shoe box. It can be placed either on top of or in the bottom of the cage, depending on whether you prefer to supervise this adventure.

Then There Are Games!

Give an intelligent African grey a moment to play mind games with you. It'll prove who really is the smartest creature on earth! Take advantage of your companion's inventiveness and keen observation skills.

Interactive games: Repeat every sound your grey makes, exactly like it makes them. The objective is to see how many sounds you can repeat. This game can also be played from room to room, as a contact call game. Then switch the game. Create the sounds for your parrot to repeat.

Physical ball (wiffle) games: Nothing is more precious than to watch a grey chick waddle across the floor to fetch a rolling ball. Some play sophisticated games. They have to toss a ball into a cup to outscore their human companions. Another grey favorite is called "watch the human." The parrot drops the ball or toy off the cage. It watches the human fetch it. Sometimes they like to play this game with the family dogs.

Name games: "What's that?" is a popular game for teaching parts of body and objects in the room. "What's that? Foot . . . Good bird!"

Baby games: The ever-popular peek-a-boo is one of the most popular African Grey games. "Where's Sweet Pea? Peek-a-boo!"

Towel games: Avian behavior consultant Sally Blanchard believes owners should teach their parrots to be comfortable with towels. It is important for them to feel relaxed, when toweled for emergencies and veterinarian visits. She says that many parrots become afraid of towels because people cover the birds by swooping the towels down over their heads. This can trigger a fear-of-predator-from-above reaction.

Games can help alleviate fears of towels. At night, Merlin loves to bite at, hide under, and play peek-a-boo with a towel on top of her sleeping cage. Some greys like to grab onto the towels with their beaks. Then they love to be gently swung and then cuddled in them.

Introducing the towel: As with toys, introduce the towel slowly. Spend a few days or weeks playing with the towel yourself. When your grey is curious, let it beak the towel. Once it is comfortable with the towel, place the parrot on the towel. Slowly wrap the towel around your bird. But do not come from above its head.

Teaching to Shower

1. Bring your grey into the bathroom while you're taking a shower. Place it on top of your shower curtain rod, or on a shower perch. If it appears nervous, place it on a portable perch in another part of the bathroom, such as by the bathroom mirror. Many greys love to beak the gray-colored birdies in the mirror. Let it observe you having lots of fun. Move around under the shower. Sing. Cluck. Shake the water off your body. Laugh. Depending on your bird, you may consider gently throwing a little water its way with your hands. Avoid getting water in its eyes, ears and cere (nose). Follow this procedure until you feel it is ready for the next step.

2. Turn your shower head to its most delicate speed, preferably a mist. Hold your parrot on your hand. Let it watch you play with the water. Make funny sounds. Giggle. Encourage your grey to beak at the water with you.

3. Once it is comfortable with this procedure, the next step is to introduce it to the spray. I let my greys lean against my chest while wetting different parts of their bodies.

Make sure the bathroom is warm and there are no drafts. Some owners dry their birds in towels. Others use hair dryers. If you use a hair dryer, keep it at a safe distance from your parrot. Be careful about which ones you use. Many hair dryers are coated with PTFE nonstick coating, which can be dangerous when heated (see Before Bringing Your Grey Home). The best alternative is to let your bird dry as nature intended, naturally.

A steam bath is very good for healthy skin and feathers; so I let my greys "hang out" in the bathroom with me every morning. I only shower them twice a week.

The Bathtub

Some greys prefer bathtubs or sinks, so that they can play in the water. After your bird becomes comfortable in the bathroom, place some of its toys in the tub. Let it observe you kneeling and playing happily with the toys.

When it becomes curious, place your bird in the back of the tub to play with the toys. Let water run lightly out of the faucet. As your bird becomes more comfortable, gently brush some water toward it and the toys. Play with the water with your hands. Wet the top of your bird's feet. As your parrot becomes more comfortable, put the stopper in the tub. Raise the water level no higher than one and one-half inches, so that it can play in the water. Never leave your bird unattended.

The Spray Bath and Other Alternatives

Some greys enjoy being sprayed by water bottles. They prefer the spray to be as light or misty as possible. The spray bottle also should be introduced in increments.

To discover which bathing alternative works best for your parrot, try different variations and make small adjustments with location, type of bath, strength of spray, and so on.

No Shoulders

The shoulder is an unsafe place for a young grey, especially a clumsy one. It is difficult to hold onto a shoulder, and a few hard falls to the floor could cause injury, or possible phobia. Also, it can be unsafe for the owner, if the parrot is nippy. Sometimes parrots lightly nip at each other as a part of allopreening (mutual preening). This is not usually dangerous to them because they are protected by feathers. However, if your grey instinctively nips at you, it could damage a cheek or eye.

Do not allow your grey on your shoulder, unless it has been trained to sit there quietly without biting. It should only be allowed when you *choose* to put it there.

Broadcasting

African greys feel more secure when they know what is going to happen next. Avian behavior consultant Gail Langsner taught me a simple technique called "broadcasting." It involves explaining to the bird what will transpire, before it happens. For example, if you want to move your parrot from its cage to a window perch, say the following: "Want perch (pointing to window perch)? Let's go to perch . . . Up . . . Good bird! . . . Here's the perch . . . Down . . . Good bird!"

Once your parrot becomes comfortable in its surroundings, it will probably begin broadcasting to you where it wants to go. The cues may be verbal or body language, such as crouching in the direction in which it wants to go, or tapping the water bowl when it wants a bath. The more opportunities your grey has to feel that it is controlling its environment, the happier it will be. Read its body language. Listen to its cues. Let it know that you understand. "Do you want to come out? Do you want perch? Do you want toy box?"

Remember that, in the wild, a prey bird, especially a partial ground-feeding one, will probably be dead, if it is caught off guard. The concept of broadcasting minimizes surprises. At the same time, it allows the parrot to have a sense of control.

Bird Sitters

For times when you must go away, you may need to find a sitter for your bird. There are two parts to this equation: finding a qualified sitter and preparing your parrot.

A Qualified Sitter

Check with your veterinarian, bird club, bird friends, breeder, or local birdstore for possible recommendations for a good sitter. The sitter should have experience caring for greys. Spend time at the facility to interview the sitter. Check out the cleanliness and care procedures. Here are some guidelines:

✔ A good sitter will have a policy of requiring veterinarian check-ups before boarding the parrot.

✔ How many parrots does the sitter take in at one time?

✔ How often and long are the birds allowed out of their cages?

✔ How often and long are they played with?

✔ What are they fed?

✔ Do you feel safe leaving your grey companion with this person?

✔ If there are emergencies, is the sitter qualified to handle them?

An alternative to using a professional sitter may be to create a "buddy system" with a trusted parrot owner friend to keep each other's greys while either one of you is away. Ask yourself the above questions before entrusting the care of your companion to anyone.

Another alternative may be to have a qualified person come by your home on a daily basis to feed and work with your grey. This will depend on the length of time you will be away, the size of your flock, and the demeanor and age of your bird, among other things. Since greys are social flock birds by nature, it is best not to leave them alone in your home.

The best alternative may be to leave your grey at home with a spouse or other family member who has been trained to handle your bird. This is the least disruptive alternative. It gives less-favored-humans a chance to develop relationships with the bird.

Preparing Your Grey

You know that you will be away only for a few days and that the facility or person you chose is qualified. But, your parrot has a different perspective. Greys, particularly young ones a year or younger, view being left behind as abandonment by the flock. Many greys have turned phobic a few days or weeks after they were left behind while their owners went on vacation. Accordingly, the manner in which you prepare it makes all the difference.

✔ Weeks before taking vacation, take your bird over to the facility. Spend the afternoon there. Walk around the place holding your bird. Introduce it to the sitter. Go off for an hour or so to do an errand. This gives time for the bird and sitter to get acquainted.

✔ A few days later, let your grey spend a night there. Tell it you'll be back the next day. You may choose to do this a few times before departure.

✔ Prepare your parrot for the stay beforehand. Tell it how much fun it will have. Take a few of its favorite perches and toys to the place, as well as special foods. While you're away, call frequently to talk to it over the phone, so that it knows it was not abandoned.

✔ If you're leaving your feathered companion with less-favored-family members, give the people opportunities to bond before you go on vacation.

Take Your Grey with You

Another alternative may be to take your grey with you, if you have the time to spend with it. Travel away from home, including outings about town, provides opportunities to build a stronger relationship with your bird. However, it must be introduced in increments. The parrot must always feel safe.

✔ Before taking your grey on vacation, acclimate it first to travel around the block and visits with friends. Think through potential problems that may scare your parrot and how to work through them. For example, I helped Merle work through her fears of the windshield wipers and going through tunnels.

✔ Plan ahead. Make reservations early because many hotels will not accept animal companions. Airlines allow only one animal per cabin. If you're planning to visit a friend, send a small cage ahead of time.

✔ Always keep a current health certificate on hand because most airports are strict about health codes. Check with your air carrier.

✔ Greys out of territory need the security and reassurances of the human companion. Therefore, it is important to be physically with your parrot, when you're on a trip. If you plan to leave it alone all day, leave it at home instead. Never leave your parrot alone in a hotel room. There have been thefts. If you're staying with a friend or relative, it is easier to leave it alone for short periods, but check in frequently.

[1]D'Arezzo, Carol, and Lauren Shannon-Nunn. *A Practical Guide to Parrot Toys and Play Areas*. Crow Fire Publishing, Springfield, Virginia. 2000, p. 17.

One aspect of helping your new companion feel secure is proper handling. A wobbly parrot is an insecure one that will not trust its new owner. Greys need to be able to grip onto something to feel stable. But if one is forced to sit on its owner's arm or the back of a hand, it is not secure because it is not able to grip its feet around something. The proper way to hold a new parrot is on the top two fingers of a hand so that its toes grip around the fingers.

How to Hold: Tuck your thumb into the palm of your hand. Hold your four fingers together, as in the *four sign.* Hold your hand horizontal so that your forefinger is the top finger and your palm faces your stomach. Fold in your bottom two fingers. Slightly bend your top fingers. Your grey should perch on your top fingers.

If your bird feels wobbly on your fingers, pull your arm close in to your waist so that it has the security of leaning against your body while learning to sit on your fingers. Take at least ten minutes every day to sit quietly with your parrot on your hand. This will help it feel more secure and stabilized.

Up/Down Commands

It is important that your parrot learn to consistently get onto and off your fingers on command, in case there are emergencies when you need to move it immediately. The *up/down* commands are useful tools.

Place the back of your hand slightly below your grey's midbreast. Say *"Up."* If it does not respond, gently press against its breast. Say *"Up"* again. When it steps up onto your fingers, slowly move your hand forward (into the bird's breast) and up, in an arc, to pick up the bird. Say *"Good bird!!!"*

If it does not step up, gently place its foot onto your fingers. Say *"Up."* Push your hand forward and up, in an arc, to pick it up. Get really excited and say *"Good bird!!!"*

To put your bird back on the perch, place your hand slightly below the crossbar, so that your grey's breast is parallel to the bar. Say *"Down"* and gently roll your hand forward (toward the perch) so that the bird is encouraged to step up onto the crossbar.

Tip: To pick up, make sure the back of your hand is slightly below your grey's midbreast so that it must *step*

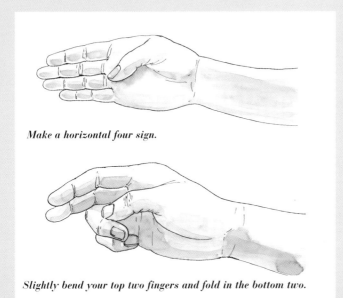

Make a horizontal four sign.

Slightly bend your top two fingers and fold in the bottom two.

GREY

up. If your hand is too far away, or below the bird's feet, it may either ignore you or bend down to bite you. When putting it back on the perch, the parrot's breast should be parallel to the crossbar so that it actually is *stepping up* to get back onto the perch when you say *"Down."*

Stick Training: It always is a good idea to have a parrot stick trained, in case it becomes difficult to handle or an insecure bird handler must work with it. The first step is to make sure your parrot is comfortable with the dowel (stick). Play with it in front of your grey for a few days. Once it becomes curious, let it play with the stick during play time.

When your grey is comfortable with the dowel, work on the *up/down* commands with it. Place the dowel at slightly below midbreast. Say *"Up."* The moment your parrot steps up onto the stick, move it forward and up in an arc. Follow the same procedure as above when putting it back on the perch. Say *"Down."*

Tip: When getting your grey to step *down* off the stick, place the tip of the dowel under the perch crossbar so that when the parrot steps off, the stick doesn't fly up and tap the parrot's tail. I found that because the dowel is so light, it tends to jerk up from the loss of the bird's weight when it steps off.

Place the back of your hand slightly below the parrot's breast.

Secure the tip of the stick under the crossbar when placing the parrot back on the perch.

The purpose of this chapter is to briefly discuss a few behavior concepts. It is not meant to provide specific advice. Behavior is a complicated area, and each African grey is an individual with a different set of personality and behavior issues.

African greys bond with caretakers whom they trust. They respond to being consistently coached and reassured in a calm, non-aggressive manner. The key to molding a trust relationship is to understand your grey's basic nature, and to *influence* its behavior by building on its natural instincts and reactions.

The Power of Attention

Greys are so intelligent and observant that they notice everything that goes on in the household. They are notorious for studying every movement and reaction and learning what works at getting the attention of their human companions.

They study us humans down to the minute detail. Much of the time, we don't even realize it. For example, my Sweet Pea studied how I move her to a portable perch whenever she prepares to poop. Now, she pretends to need to poop when she wants to go to the perch. It took months before I noticed exactly what she was doing.

Greys are capable of simple cause-and-effect thinking. For example, Congo grey Alfie lived in

Each African grey is unique with a different set of personality and behavior issues.

the kitchen. He studied how every time the microwave oven beeped, his owner George was right there. So, Alfie started beeping like a microwave to get George's attention too. And sure enough, George came running to his cage to yell at him.

Once a grey observes that it gets attention from its behavior, it will repeat that behavior. Unfortunately, attention from its owner can be in the form of either a positive or negative reaction. When the owner continues to reinforce the behavior with the same positive or negative response, the parrot's behavior then becomes a behavior pattern.

For example, Alfie's beeping was the natural response of an intelligent, observant grey. But it became a problem to George who had little patience with the sound. George reinforced the beeping into a pattern by running over to the cage and yelling whenever Alfie beeped. He gave Alfie negative attention.

The key to working effectively with an African grey is to be clear on what kind of "attention" you are giving to your bird. For example, there was nothing wrong with Alfie imitating the microwave sound. However, it became a problem because it bothered George. But once George learned to give Alfie attention when the parrot was quiet, the beeping stopped.

Original Cause

There are many reasons why parrots act a certain way. Usually the extreme behaviors, such as biting and screaming, manifest because the caretaker was not properly reading the original cause, or the original body language attempt to communicate. For example, when Merlin Tewillager was a chick, she grabbed onto my thumb with her beak to steady herself when I picked her up. I nervously pulled away, not understanding what she was doing. Her action then grew into a bite. Accordingly, this interaction mushroomed into a behavior problem. She learned the "power of a bite" and began reacting to me with other biting behaviors. Had I figured out why she was grabbing my thumb and not overreacted, the incident may not have grown into a problem.

A grey owner complained that her five-month-old Congo was constantly begging. She was concerned that she had spoiled it because that was one of the most popular explanations that she had read. It turns out that the parrot was sick with a yeast infection and died a few weeks later. Had she known how to read her bird by observing and questioning further what the parrot may be communicating, perhaps the bird's life could have been saved. Formula answers do not work most of the time.

The first step in changing negative behavior is to understand why the parrot behaves as it does and here is how:
- Start a log.
- When, how often, and where does the interaction happen?
- What do you do and how does your grey respond?
- What is your reaction?
- What reward is the parrot getting from this behavior?

- What is its body language telling you?
- If there is any doubt, *always* have your parrot checked out by an avian veterinarian.

Working on Negative Behaviors

Greys do not respond well to punishment. Tactics, such as squirting, covering the cage, or putting the bird in a dark closet can quickly unravel any trust relationship. They can possibly trigger an insecure grey into becoming even more nervous and perhaps phobic. Do not ever hit, throw, or drop your parrot on the floor. Wobbling (shaking the hand holding the bird to distract it from biting) can be devastating to an insecure grey. A gentle wobble does not even work with a more stable, observant grey. That's because it only takes a few shakes for the parrot to figure out how to hold on, while still biting the hand. Strategies utilizing domination or force can damage the relationship. All it takes is one fearful incident to trigger the parrot into viewing its owner as a predator, even if the relationship had been strong prior to the situation. So, what does work?

Positive Reinforcement

Reward your bird for doing what you want it to do. A reward can be in the form of a treat, praise, head scratch, or an activity, such as moving to a favorite perch. For example, if your grey does not want to go into the cage at night, place a treat in the cage so that your parrot wants to go in there for it.

Behavior consultant Jane Hallander believes that some behavior strategies do not work because they lack the reward.[1] The objective is to get your bird to do what you want it to do because it "wants" to do it. Use treats to begin the positive behavior. Once the pattern is in place, the reward can be transferred to praise or a head scratch. Use treats that your bird does not get very often.

Inaccessibility

Use common sense. If you do not want your parrot to chew your window sill, do not place it there. If you do not want it to chew your necklace, take the necklace off or position the bird so that it cannot reach it. Placing a parrot at the point of temptation (on the window sill) and demanding that it not do what its natural tendency is to do (chew the wood), does not work.

Redirecting Behavior

Confrontation with a grey does not work. Observe situations that may cause confrontation. Then identify ways to redirect the behavior by adding a reward. For example, demanding that a reluctant parrot get on your hand to come out of the cage deteriorates the trust relationship. However, if you can give it a reason for wanting to come out (reward), both of you will have a win-win situation. Again, the reward may be a treat or the opportunity to go to another room with you.

Distraction

Many behavior consultants recommend distraction techniques for redirecting negative behaviors. For example, if you are holding a parrot that's biting you, hold a small object off to the side in your other hand and shake it to distract the bird. It may be a toy, napkin, or any small object nearby. Just shaking your hand below the bird may be enough to redirect attention. Making quick sounds, doing something silly, or making a quick body movement can also distract.

These techniques are meant only to distract and not to frighten the bird. Do not use objects that may scare the parrot. Do not hold objects or your hand above the bird's head because this could trigger a sensitive grey into a fear-of-predator situation.

The Neutral Room

Birds are protective of their territories. But when they are in a neutral area (out of their territory), they are less aggressive. Avian behavior consultant Sally Blanchard recommends working with your parrot in a neutral room (room that the parrot does not consider to be its territory), particularly when you are working on behavior skills, such as the *up/down* commands.[2] Use of the neutral room allows an unsure owner to gain confidence since the parrot is calmer in the neutral room (away from its territory). Introduce the parrot slowly to the new room.

Working on Yourself

Greys notice every detail in our body language, as well as our reactions to them. Therefore, it is important to be aware of our interactions in order to reward positive behavior, instead of reacting to a negative behavior.

They are so attuned to us that it is almost as if they read our minds. Sometimes when we have a fear that something may happen, we reflect that fear in our body language. An observant grey will pick up on it. For example, if you're afraid your parrot is going to bite and have a mental image of your bird biting you, your demeanor will change. Your parrot will most likely read your apprehensive body language, and bite you.

Learn to read your grey's body language.

However, a technique called "visualization" can help you change the mental picture to a positive image. For example, if you visualize your bird stepping up onto your hand without biting, you feel more relaxed. You carry yourself confidently, which sets the tone of your body language.

A fear or anger reaction to a parrot will result either in a fearful or aggressive reaction to you. For this reason, behavior consultants recommend that you step back from a heated moment of confrontation. Calm your energy and focus clearly on the situation. The best reaction to a negative behavior is *no reaction.* Leave the room. Return when both of you have calmed down. Redirect the interaction between you and your grey by rewarding good behavior.

Introducing Less-Favored Persons

Greys in the wild get along with many personalities. Although they have a favored mate, they are capable of moving on to another if their mate dies. In the home, they are capable of forming relationships with all members of the household. The manner in which they are introduced will make a difference in how the parrot responds to other members.

✔ From the beginning, make sure all household members that want a relationship with the parrot begin working with the bird. Delegate specific activities.

✔ Do not react or take it personally if the parrot prefers another household member. An

Greys are sensitive creatures and they do not respond well to punishment and control techniques.

Reward your parrot for positive behavior by giving it a treat that it enjoys, but does not get very often.

═══ **CHECKLIST** ═══

Ideas for Avoiding Biting Situations

✔ Read your grey's body language.
  • Are its eyes pinning?
  • Are the feathers on its back standing up?
  • Does it push your hand away with its beak when it does not want to be petted or scratched?

✔ Work around situations when it normally bites.
  • If it bites while you're on the telephone, put it on a perch before using the phone.
  • If it nips while you're cleaning or putting food in the cage, remove it from the cage first.

✔ If it bites because it does not want to do something, redirect the behavior. Positively reward so that it wants to do it.
  • If it bites to avoid getting off your hand, place its favorite treat on the cage so that it wants to get off your hand to retrieve the treat. Good bird!

angry or competitive reaction to the parrot will conjure a confrontational reaction.

✔ The parrot is calmer when the favored person is out-of-sight because it does not have to protect its bonded companion (or mate in the wild). Therefore, the less-favored person should work with the parrot while the favored one is away, such as on a trip or doing errands. If the favored person is at home, he/she should take the parrot to a neutral room and allow the less-favored person to work alone with the bird.

✔ The less-favored person should give the grey its favorite treats.

Screaming

Wild parrots that are separated from each other make contact calls back and forth to keep in touch. When one does not respond, it usually means that it is dead. In the home, when the human companion leaves the room, the grey calls out as its instinctive fear of being left behind arises. If the companion does not respond, it calls louder. Eventually, the calling turns into a scream. The human response may be to scream back, or to run to the cage to yell at the bird, or to cover it up. Either way, the parrot has observed that its scream gets a reaction (attention reward). The solution: take the parrot with you from room to room. If you are not able to do that, tell it you are leaving and "will be back." Make whistles back and forth every once in a while between rooms.

There are many other reasons why parrots scream:

✔ It may be afraid of something, such as a new object in the room, a new cage or playpen. If you've recently moved, it may be nervous about the change in environment.
✔ It may be hungry.
✔ It may enjoy making the sound.

If your grey screams, look for the *original* cause and identify ways to redirect to positive behavior.

The contact calling game: Merlin Tewillager learned how much fun the cockatoo scream was to make. On top of that, it drove me crazy. Therefore, I turned the activity into a game.

Every time she screamed, I responded with a softer sound that my ears could handle. Eventually, she began replicating the new sound. The cockatoo scream disappeared.

Biting Behavior

The first step in avoiding a biting behavior problem is to not expect it. Visualize a well-behaved grey companion that steps up onto your hand without biting. Greys in the wild seldom bite. Greys in the home do not bite if their caretakers properly read their body language and know how to avoid situations where they may bite.

If your grey bites, pinpoint the *original cause*.

✔ Insecurity and fear can trigger a parrot to bite. Many grey owners have biting problems with their parrots because they are not handling them properly. Does your grey feel secure on your hand? Is it able to grip its feet around your fingers? Is it grabbing on to your thumb to secure itself?

✔ Sometimes biting is hormonal. If your grey is nippy during mating season, watch its body language closely. Avoid contact when it displays.

✔ Some greys are known for nipping at the fingers of their bonded companions, while being preened. Every night Sweet Pea lowers her head to be preened. If I hit a sensitive spot, she lets out a sensitive nip.

✔ Greys may bite while defending their territories, such as their cages, toys, playboxes, favorite perches, and so on. They are also known for defending their mates (bonded companions) from intruders. Their definition of intruders may include the rest of the family. They may nip at the intruders. But sometimes

TIP

The African Grey Sucker Ploy

Recognize this? You put your hand in the cage and say *"Up."* But your grey puts its head down for a scratch. The moment you begin to rubs its head, it reaches around and gives you a big nip! Avian behavior consultant Liz Wilson calls it the "sucker punch."[3] A grey that puts its head down for a scratch but is "looking up out of the corner of its eye" is usually preparing to bite. A grey that truly wants its head scratched usually closes its eyes or is looking down.

The solution: Give it a reason to want to climb onto your hand. Again, the reward can be food, a toy, praise, or an activity, such as coming out for a head scratch. Distraction techniques, such as shaking your other hand off to the side, can help to deflect attention.

A grey with its head down for a scratch, but looking up is waiting for a sucker to bite.

Most feather picking problems stem from physical causes.

Visualize a well-behaved bird that steps up without biting.

the biting is displaced onto the mate because the parrot cannot reach the intruders.

✔ Sometimes they bite as a reaction to what is going on in their caretakers' lives. If the caretaker has had a bad day, or feels stressed and is not giving proper attention to his parrot, he can expect a nip.

✔ Once a grey learns the reward of a bite and that biting is reinforced with the attention it wants, it may continue the biting pattern until its behavior is redirected.

Dealing with a Bite

Try *not* to react when your parrot bites. Usually the first nip is not too severe. Sometimes

It takes time and practice to become good at preening.

the parrot is only grabbing at your hand with its beak. However, once you pull away, either the initial grip gets stronger, or the second lunge is more severe.

Feather Picking

Feather picking is one of the most dreaded problems of African grey owners. First, it is not a pretty sight to see a parrot with mutilated feathers. Secondly, the misconception that most feather picking is due to boredom incorrectly gives the impression that the owner is a bad caretaker. The owner then becomes embarrassed. This adds to any insecurity the grey may be feeling that "something is wrong with me, something is wrong with the flock." The fact is, that the majority of feather-picking problems stem from physical causes.

First, there are different types of feather picking. Some parrots bite or snip parts of their feathers. Sometimes they chew or shred the feathers. Others totally pull out their feathers, right down to the bare skin. This is called feather plucking. No matter the type of picking, nothing can be more devastating than to wake up one day to discover one's cherished companion naked with a pile of feathers on the bottom of the cage.

If this happens, the first thing to do is to get an avian veterinarian check-up. This is not a time to save money by limiting the types of testing because the picking will continue until the original cause of the picking is uncovered. In addition to a regular health check-up, additional tests for problems, such as giardia, aspergillosis, and metal toxicity (particularly zinc), should be considered. Additional areas of testing may be discussed with the veterinarian,

such as other possible bacterial infections that may relate to your home and neighborhood. Other physical problems may relate to nutritional deficiencies, such as calcium, vitamin A, or fatty acids.

In a period of devastating weather changes and disasters, environmental factors may be a culprit. Aspergillus, for example, is a common slow-growing fungus that can be found in the soil, moldy food, and cage-bottom materials, such as corncob bedding and ground walnut shells. In areas experiencing extreme rainfall, it may be even more prevalent. Its spores spread throughout the air and can attack parrots' air sacs, causing a disease called aspergillosis. Even in drier areas, aspergillus spores can attack parrots with compromised immune systems and other nutritional deficiencies.

In areas of drought and low humidity, greys may suffer from dry skin and react by snipping off and plucking feathers. Humidifiers should be used in periods of dryness, particularly in the winter when wood stoves and other heaters are operating. Humidifiers are discussed in Before Bringing Your Grey Home.

When the cause of feather picking is psychological, it usually is due to a fear reaction to something, such as being left alone. When you have a big change in your life, such as a new job, baby, or home, be conscientious about making time for your grey and helping it through the changes.

First Cause/Second Cause

Do not overreact if your parrot feather picks because once it realizes how a snip-of-the-beak gets to you, it may manipulate you with this behavior. Even if the original cause that related to a physical problem is resolved, it may continue feather picking, if you had demonstrated any kind of overconcern during the treatment. The behavior becomes a pattern. Then it turns into a behavior problem. Here are tips for changing it.

✔ Do not yell at the bird.

✔ Do not run over to cover the cage.

✔ Do not give it any kind of attention reward when it picks.

✔ Do not react at all.

✔ Do not think about it.

✔ Do not worry about it.

✔ Do not focus on the problem at all, including pretending your bird is fully feathered because it signifies that you are concerned. Just leave the room when it picks.

Place a mirror in the cage. It serves as a cage mate and allows the bird to cuddle up with another parrot of its kind. Introduce the mirror as you would introduce a new toy. Some people purchase additional parrots for companionship. This usually backfires, and the parrot may pluck even more, due to jealousy of the newcomer.

Provide many chew toys that keep your companion busy, such as shredders.

Finding the Right Avian Behavior Consultant

We have lots of experience nurturing domesticated animals, like dogs and cats; but relating to a parrot for the first time can be overwhelming, especially one as smart and sensitive as an African grey. That is why it is important to read everything you can about the species. Talk with as many bird owners as possible. Use your judgment and common sense to weed through the conflicting attitudes and behavior strategies. The moment you feel a problem arising, look for a qualified avian behavior consultant and find out important information, such as:

✔ What is the consultant's overall philosophy about working with parrots?

✔ What is his/her track record in working specifically with African greys?

✔ How long has he/she been a consultant? How did he/she learn the trade?

✔ Does the consultant appear to have a rapport with your parrot?

✔ Does the consultant have a gentle working style?

✔ What do other grey owners say about the consultant?

[1]Hallander, Jane, Interview, July, 2000.

[2]Blanchard, Sally, *Companion Parrot Handbook*. Pet Bird Information Council; Alameda, California, 1999, p. 158.

[3]Wilson, Liz, "Biting: The Great Power Game," *Grey Play Round Table*. Tewillager Publishing, division of Equatorial Group, Ltd.; Old Chatham, New York, Spring 1996, p. 3.

REHABILITATING GREYS

The probability is high that every African grey will live in more than one household during its lifetime, given its potential life span of up to sixty years or older. Therefore, there will be a glut of grey parrots needing new homes in the near future.

Some caretakers give up their parrots because of life changes, such as new marriages, children, or jobs. Others give them up because they are no longer interested in having them. Whatever the reason, being moved to a new flock can be an ordeal for any grey, no matter the previous circumstances. Being moved into a new home (new territory) can be terrifying. Therefore, the new arrival needs to feel loved, accepted, and secure as quickly as possible.

The Behavior Tunnel

Some greys begin an early career of being passed from home to home. Breeder Phoebe Linden believes many fall into a process she describes as a "behavior tunnel."[1] Somewhere between the ages of one and two, young parrots experience an adolescent phase. As discussed in Getting to Know Your Grey, they may test and challenge their caregivers. Not only are they learning how to get along with other flockmates at this time in the wild, but they are also experiencing initial hormonal and sexual impulses. Therefore, in captivity, this is a

Older greys make wonderful companions.

confusing time when they need direction and instruction.

But unfortunately some become behavior problems. They may become intolerant of all people except a favored human. They may become increasingly terrified of new toys, objects, and situations. Or, they may adopt negative behavior patterns, such as biting or screaming. Their caretakers may be unclear on how to work with them. As a result, they deviate into restricted lives where they are confined to their cages most of the time, or sold or given away.

They enter their new homes, and unless they have been lucky enough to find a new owner willing to work through the previously reinforced behavior issues, they may be passed on, time after time.

Older Wild-Caught Greys

Although wild-caught greys have not been sold in the United States since 1993, there are many currently living in captivity that often need new homes. They probably are cage-bound and are fed primarily sunflower seed and peanut diets. Their owners probably had purchased them before the infusion of avian care information on the market.

Death of an Owner

Some greys are in need of new homes because their beloved favored humans have passed on. If their owners had helped them adjust to the possibility of a new home by teaching them to accept others and exposing them to new places and adventures, the adjustment to a new home may be less difficult. However, if they did not, these parrots may experience a traumatic adjustment to a new home.

With the right care and love, all of the greys mentioned above can make irreplaceable family companions. If you choose to adopt a grey that needs a new home, here are some pointers:

Quarantine: As discussed in Before Bringing Your Grey Home, the new grey must be quarantined from the rest of the flock.

Two-week window: The grey is entering new territory. It probably will be compliant for approximately two weeks before learning its way around the house. This window of time allows you to observe the bird and set up daily patterns.

One increment at a time: Greys adjust to change, one increment at a time. Being in a new territory (home) is a big increment. Therefore, keep everything else as familiar as possible, while it adjusts. For example, keep it in its old cage, even if it is small. Maintain its diet as close to the original as possible, until it appears to be adjusting to your home. After it has adjusted, introduce the larger cage, diet, and other changes slowly.

Positive reinforcement: Identify treats it loves. Praise and reward it often. Positive, reassuring words are crucial. Let it know how happy you are to have it in the new flock. When I keep nervous greys at my house, I sit with them for a few minutes after my own parrots have gone to bed. I tell them how special they are. Sometimes I stick my head under the cage covers at night to talk softly with them.

Building trust: Remember that your new companion has gone through other owners. It may take time to build trust. Depending on the temperament and history of the bird, it may be terrified of every movement that goes on . . . every time you bring food . . . every time you change the papers. Therefore, make sure its cage is placed in a corner. Cover a section with a towel so that it can feel safe. Sit in the room with your new companion, as often as possible. Talk in a soft, calm voice. At the same time, feel love and compassion in your heart for this nervous little creature.

Regression feeding: In the wild, birds that are nervous do not eat because the movement may attract predators. Therefore, in captivity, a nervous parrot in a new territory will instinctively eat less. Either spoonfeed or feed pureed foods to the bird with your fingers, in addition to its regular food (see Teaching Your Grey to Eat a Balanced Diet). If the parrot is very nervous, serve it through the cage bars.

The Case of Laurie

Laurie was a 20-year-old wild-caught Congo grey. He had lived in a filthy cage, too small for a Pionus. His diet consisted of sunflower seeds, corn, and peanuts. He had been originally purchased by a man who later left him with his mother who eventually died. He was a frightened, cage-bound feather picker. He was a biter, screamer, and he swore. He had fits if the lights were not out at eight o'clock on the nose. He was terrified of gloves and sticks.

His cage had a padlocked door. He was virtually unhandleable.

The son eventually brought him to a pet store to find a home. A *Grey Play Round Table* magazine subscriber named Margaret agreed to work with him. The first step was to take him to the veterinarian's office for a check-up. Laurie became so frantic that the veterinarian had to give him oxygen. His physical condition was so poor that they decided to forgo a blood test. There were no other birds at Margaret's house; therefore, an at-home quarantine was unnecessary.

Margaret and her teenage daughter Steph teamed up to work with Laurie. Margaret would be the trainer. Steph was the socializer. After Laurie had been in the home for a week, all peanuts and favorite foods were removed from his diet. He was only given them by hand, in preparation for hand training and positive reinforcement. Margaret put a training perch in front of the cage door with a peanut in the food cup. Eventually Laurie came out of the cage to eat the peanuts. After a few days of these peanut feedings, Margaret calmly whisked Laurie and the perch into the bathroom away from his cage (territory).

The bathroom was then used as the neutral room for teaching the *up/down* commands. She sat on the floor with Laurie. She talked soothingly. She gently touched his breast and placed her hand in front of his breast for step-ups. In spite of thrashing, screaming, and biting attacks, Laurie finally sat on her hand panting. He was rewarded with several peanuts and praise. The following days consisted of repeat performances, but each time, Laurie was a little calmer.

All the while, Steph had been playing the good-guy socializer. She sat by the cage, calmly talking to him, feeding him, and just spending time alone in the room with him. Laurie would call for Steph and ask for head scratches through the cage. She could feed him new foods. She provided stability and joy in his life while undergoing the stressful training period.

Laurie was then moved into the living room. Margaret held back the training sessions for a few days to allow the parrot time to adjust to this new increment (the new room). At this point he was consistently jumping on and off Margaret and Steph's hands and spending quiet times sitting on their hands. As he became confident, they began slowly walking around the room with the bird on their hands. Steph was then able to take Laurie to the kitchen to help her, and to her bedroom to hang out, while Steph did her homework.

Finally, Laurie was taken back to the veterinarian for a physical exam. The veterinarian was visibly choked up when she made the connection that this calm, healthy African grey was the same ill, hysterical bird that she had to put on oxygen one year ago, after attempting an earlier exam.

Romeo's Reactions

Romeo was a two-year-old domestically raised Congo grey. His owner Sharon had given him lots of love and guidance. But one day he snapped. Every time she came into the room he screamed, growled, thrashed against the bars, and then cowered in the corner of the cage. Sometimes he threw himself on the bottom of the cage, laid on his back, and shook his feet and claws, as if defending himself to the end. She could feel the terror and pain in this bird's heart.

The problem was that Sharon had track lighting installed on the living room ceiling.

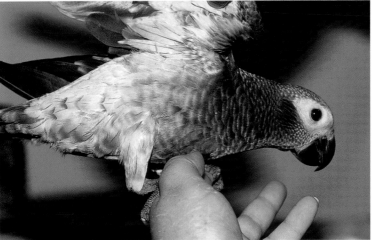

Above left: Make changes one increment at a time.

Above right: Regression feeding helps a new companion feel more secure.

Left: Up/down commands were worked on in a neutral room.

Above left: Make sure your parrot's wings and nails are not clipped too short.

Above right: View situations through the parrot's perspective.

Right: Reward your grey with its favorite treats.

She had neglected to remove Romeo while the workmen installed the lights. To Romeo, the room (his territory) was being invaded, not only by strangers, but also by scary hawks (the lights) that looked down on him from the ceiling. Romeo associated this terrifying experience with Sharon. Ever since that day, he become phobic (terrified) of her presence.

The trigger that makes a grey terrified and fearful is not always apparent. Sometimes it is something simple, as a part of a series of events that builds up. It can range from an encounter of watching a wild bird through the window being attacked by a hawk to the vibration from an earthquake. Sometimes it is from something physical, such as a broken wing or blood feather, or a terrifying encounter at the veterinarian's office. Other phobic reactions have arisen after the parrot is left behind when the owner goes on vacation. One of the most common triggers for phobic reactions is when a grey's wings and nails are clipped too short. It falls off the cage, and the worried owner then rushes over and chases the bird to comfort it.

The caretaker is then associated as the predator and the bird becomes terrified at the person's presence. This does not mean that parrots become phobic because their owners are mean. The parrot mind works differently from the human mind. A perception of betrayal does not necessarily mean it really happened.

Avoiding Phobic Reactions

If your grey is confident and secure, chances are it will not turn phobic. However, it still is necessary to follow certain procedures to help it remain secure.

✔ Expose it safely and in increments to new experiences. Avoid wing and toe nail clips that are too short.

✔ If you go on vacation, follow the guidelines outlined in Teaching Your Grey Everyday Living Skills.

✔ View situations from the parrot's perspective. When changes are being made to its territory, remove it during the changes. Then reintroduce it slowly to the new room or home. Whenever my greys and I move, I take them over to the new house in stages of moving, so that they are comfortable when we physically move in.

✔ If your bird falls to the floor, do not chase it. Wait until it looks over to you to be picked up.

✔ Do not chase your parrot, even if you are just playing a game. There have been instances where greys have acted phobic the day following a night of playing chasing games with it. Instead, let it chase you.

Steps for Helping Nervous, Phobic Greys

Nothing can be more devastating than to have a cherished feathered companion become terrified of you. The first step is to not blame yourself. Act in as nonthreatening a manner as possible.

✔ Avoid direct eye contact. This can be threatening to a frightened creature. Prey birds have eyes on the side of their heads, as do most prey animals. Predators' eyes are on the front of their faces. Therefore, look at the bird from an angle, as a prey bird would. Also, keep your eyes downcast.

✔ When you enter the room, do not walk directly up to the cage. Approach it from an indirect diagonal.

✔ Sit below the cage, if possible, so that the parrot feels higher than you. Talk sweetly. Read softly. Sing lullabies. Tell it how much you love it.

✔ Never force it to do anything. Leave the cage door open when you are in the room. Then let it come out on its own. Praise it. Give it treats when it makes a breakthrough, such as coming out of the cage or putting its head down for you to scratch through the bars.

✔ Always work in increments. Be patient. It may take months, even years, for it to come around.

✔ Encourage other members of the household to work with it. Sometimes phobic birds bond with others whom they do not associate as being the predator. If your grey then bonds with another household member, try not to become jealous. This may not last forever.

[1]Linden, Phoebe. *Abundantly Avian: the Compiled Works of Phoebe Linden from The Pet Bird Report.* Santa Barbara Bird Farm, Santa Barbara, California, 1999, p. 119.

Helping a Previously Owned Grey Adjust

You may acquire your African grey through resale from a local pet store or through adoption from a relative, friend, or rescue organization. No matter how you acquire a previously owned grey parrot, you should make every effort to help it feel safe and secure in its new surroundings.

✔ Leave a towel or blanket over part of the cage for the first few days.

✔ Set the cage at chest level, and adjust its height until the bird seems more comfortable.

✔ Locate the cage within the living area but avoid areas of heavy traffic.

✔ Take your grey to an avian veterinarian for a full examination.

✔ Begin interactions with your previously owned grey cautiously and in a nonthreatening manner. It's best to start off with no direct eye contract.

✔ Seek your veterinarian's advice before attempting to improve your bird's diet.

TEACHING YOUR GREY
TO EAT A BALANCED DIET

Many grey owners are concerned about how to feed their birds the most healthful diets. There is no exact formula for feeding companion parrots. The field of avian nutrition is new and no one has all the answers.

In her book, *A Guide to a Naturally Healthy Parrot,* holistic avian health consultant, Alicia McWatters, Ph.D., C.N.C., says, "There are no universally accepted requirements for specific nutrients for birds. Although all birds require the same nutrients, each species (or individual) may require more or less of a particular nutrient, such as one that may require a higher or lower level of fat, protein, carbohydrate, vitamins, minerals, or water in their diet, and their caloric needs will vary. . . . The amount of nutrients required by an individual bird is also influenced by its age, species, size, sex, environment, activity level, stress, illness/injury, hormonal status, nutritional status, and the type of diet consumed (its bioavailability). Additionally, because each bird is biochemically and genetically unique, with different strengths and weaknesses, their quantitative nutritional needs will vary."[1]

Nutrition is a complicated science. It requires the knowledge of the functions of many nutrients, as well as how they interact with each other. I highly recommend two books that focus extensively on the subject: *A Guide to a Naturally Healthy Bird* by Alicia McWatters, Ph.D., C.N.C. and *Feeding Your Pet* by Petra Burgman, D.V.M. Both authors believe the best feeding approach is "moderation." Provide your grey the most balanced diet possible.

What Is a Balanced Diet?

In school we were taught that a balanced diet included eating the proper mix of vegetables, grains, fruits, and so on. This would provide us with the appropriate vitamins, minerals, proteins, and other building-block nutrients needed to build strong bodies. The same is true for parrots.

Most illnesses stem from a deficiency in vitamins, minerals, or other food substance nutrients. This results in secondary infections or other diseases. However, as long as you provide a wide variety of healthy foods from a variety of nutrient groups every day, your grey will receive a healthy, balanced diet. Never give up introducing new foods. There are many ways to prepare them.

Fresh, organic vegetables are chock full of valuable nutrients and enzymes.

Fresh, organic vegetables served in the raw live state are best because they contain the most nutrients and the needed enzymes that help maintain proper digestion.

Many people chop up vegetables individually and serve them together in a bowl. Some people steam them. Others serve only raw foods. Many of the beta carotene (vitamin A) vegetables should be lightly steamed (such as carrots), so they can be more easily digested. Foods that contain oxalic acid (such as spinach) should be served sparingly (no more than twice a week). They block the absorption of calcium in the body.

A mash diet, which is prepared by grating a wide variety of foods in a food processor, is attractive to many greys. Not only does "mashing" them disguise some of the foods your parrot will not normally eat, but it also tastes better because the process breaks down the cell walls. This allows the individual food flavors to blend. Greys like mash diets because they taste good. (If you are interested in a mash diet recipe, refer to the *Mash Diet* article by Dr. Alicia McWatters on the *www.africangreys.com* website.)

Pureed Foods

In the wild, parrots regurgitate foods to feed their young and mates. Similarly, feeding your grey pureed foods a few times per week promotes bonding and builds security. Cut a butternut squash in half. Place it skin up in a casserole dish with a small amount of water. Bake it at 350°F (175°C) for 45 minutes to an hour, until it is soft. Spoon it out. Puree with a little water. Cool and spoonfeed your parrot in the evening (a few spoonfuls only). Other puree delights include: sweet potatoes (bake until gushy, puree, and serve), carrots, and mashed potatoes. Interchange them to add variety. You can eat what your companion does not.

As discussed in Getting to Know Your Grey, new arrivals to the household normally eat less than normal. Spoonfeeding can help them feel more secure. Be patient when teaching your parrot to eat from a spoon. First spoonfeed yourself. Then get very excited and talk about how good it is. Offer some to your grey.

Tip: Never feed your grey food from your mouth. Do not let it play with your teeth. Normal bacteria in parrots is primarily gram positive and it proposes no health threat to humans. However, normal, healthy flora in people, which is primarily gram negative, can

---

TIP

Are Sunflower Seeds Okay?

There is nothing wrong with sunflower seeds, unless they comprise your parrot's entire diet. Dr. Alicia McWatters says that sunflower seeds contain many healthy nutrients, such as appreciable amounts of vitamin E, B complex, and many minerals, such as magnesium, potassium, iron, zinc, and calcium.[2] However, the downside is that they are high in fat. Therefore, feed them in small amounts, no more than one-half tablespoon per day. Overfeeding sunflower seeds may result in a fatty liver disease. Greys are approximately one pound in weight; therefore, a small amount of food may be deceptively high in fat.

CHECKLIST

Balanced Diet
✔ 50 percent vegetables
✔ 20 percent grains/beans
✔ 10 percent fruits
✔ 15 percent seeds/nuts
✔ 5 percent greens

Source: discussions with Dr. Alicia McWatters

make parrots sick. Do not even feed your parrot from the same spoon.

Pelleted Diets

It is a complicated science to identify the proper nutrient ratios for feeding parrots balanced diets. Therefore, pelleted diets were scientifically created to make nutritional combinations of foods. They make a good addition to the daily proportions of fresh, organic, wholesome foods.

Not all pelleted diets are alike. They differ in formulation, color, shape, texture, taste, smell, and method of production. Choose carefully and taste the products yourself. Avoid products with a long list of chemical ingredients, as well as artificial colors and flavors. There has not been enough research to date to prove that additives, such as food coloring and refined sugars, are not detrimental to parrots' small bodies. It is best to use a commercial food that is organically processed.

Some commercial feed companies may try to convince you their products are nutritionally complete, with little or no need for fresh food

supplementation. First, parrots are wild creatures and we have incomplete knowledge of the nutritional needs of wild grey parrots. Therefore, it is not possible for any product to be nutritionally complete. Secondly, companion parrots come from many areas of the world with different challenges, climates and vegetation; therefore, one type of pellet manufactured to serve parrot needs may not satisfy your parrot's nutritional requirements. Commercial feeds should comprise no more than 20 to 30 percent of your bird's daily feeding plan.

Teaching Your Grey to Eat Wholesome, Organic Vegetables

One of the most difficult challenges is to convince your grey to eat its vegetables. Here are some tips:

Sit beside your parrot and eat some of the foods you want to introduce. Play with the food with your fingers. Laugh and act as if you're really enjoying yourself. Make delicious chomping sounds. Talk about how yummy it is. Then offer some. It may take days or weeks, but eventually curiosity will take over. Another strategy is to act possessive about the food, until your grey becomes curious.

Greys change preferences. Sometimes they like things one way. The next day, they don't like it at all. Just like humans, they get tired of the same foods that are served in the same way. If your bird no longer likes a certain item, create new ways of serving it. It is important to experiment with every conceivable way of serving foods.

Above left: Fresh fruits should comprise approximately 10 percent of your grey's diet.

Above right: Carrot top greens are also valuable sources of nutrients.

Experiment with times of the day and locations in the cage. African grey Sammy eats his vegetables late at night. He makes numerous trips up and down from his sleeping perch to eat from the bowl.

Turn food into toys. African grey Burrdo did not like to eat carrots. That is, until his owner Dale began to twist the green carrot tops around the cage bars, like a toy. Now he devours them. Some greys like to eat their food on shish-kabob hangers made especially for parrots. However, avoid hangers with sharp hooks. Birds have had their lower beaks skewered on them.

Hide food in toys and other places in the cage. There are nut/seed holder toys that require ingenuity to dislodge the treats.

Greys like nuts and seeds, such as millet.

Cantaloupe is another favorite fruit.

Beta carotene vegetables, such as carrots, should be served daily.

Greys learn by demonstration. Set a place for it at your dinner table. Eat, be merry, and introduce your parrot to new, interesting foods.

Vitamin A Deficiencies

One of the most common deficiencies found in greys' diets is vitamin A or beta carotene. Vitamin A is essential for a healthy immune system, vision, resistance to infection, proper growth and development, maintenance of the lining of respiratory, reproductive, digestive and urinary tracts, and maintenance of the health and structure of skin. A deficiency in vitamin A can result in: allergies, sinus trouble, sneezing, susceptibility to infection, and rough, dry skin, as well as abnormal hormonal activity.

Vitamin A can be found in meat, eggs, cheese, and in the form of beta carotene in

Even when kissing your grey, do not allow its beak in your mouth.

plants. The meat, eggs, and cheese should be served in moderation, or not at all, depending on the health needs of your parrot.

Vegetable sources that provide beta carotene (transformed to vitamin A by the body) may be the best alternative. Beta carotene sources include: yellow/winter squashes, sweet potatoes/yams, carrots, alfalfa sprouts, endive,

kale, collard greens, mustard greens, turnip greens, broccoli, beet greens, chicory, chard, green peppers, chili peppers, red sweet peppers, yellow corn, dandelion greens, okra, and sugar snap peas, to name a few.

As the saying goes, "the darker the flesh (dark green/yellow-orange), the higher the beta carotene." It is important to provide beta carotene vegetables on a daily basis.

Appropriate Calcium Levels

Calcium is the predominant mineral in birds' bodies. It is essential for healthy bones, blood clotting, muscle contraction, and nerve and heart function. Most processes in the body are dependent on its availability. The absorption of calcium involves a complicated process. First, it must be accompanied by phosphorus and magnesium (2.5:1 ratio of calcium to both phosphorus and magnesium). Phosphorus is the second-most predominant mineral in birds' bodies. It is important for many physiological and biochemical reactions, such as RNA/DNA synthesis and the growth, repair and maintenance of cells. Magnesium is also involved in many metabolic processes.[3] Secondly, vitamin D3 must be present to enhance calcium's absorption from the intestine and the assimilation of phosphorus.

✔ Foods high in calcium include: egg shells (boiled and dried), low-fat yogurt, low-fat cheese, collard greens, turnip greens, mustard greens, kale, dandelion greens, and broccoli.

✔ Foods with good calcium/phosphorus ratios include: watercress, carrots, Swiss chard, and low-fat cheese.

✔ Foods high in phosphorus are grapes, cauliflower, apples, corn, almonds, sunflower seeds, and almonds.

Vitamin D3 is produced in the skin when birds are exposed to direct sunlight or ultraviolet light (full-spectrum lighting), such as OTT lights and Vitalites. Egg yolk and fish oils are also sources of vitamin D3.

Greys are sensitive to inadequate levels of calcium. Those with low-calcium diets often have low blood calcium. This can result in seizures, brittle bones, and poor egg formation. An imbalance with the other nutrients can result in other problems. Therefore, it is a good idea to have your grey's blood calcium levels checked intermittently in its health exams.

Merlin and Sweet Pea's Daily Meal Plan

✔ **Early morning breakfast** is a favorite meal they call "cereal'k." It consists of a half tablespoon of Arrowhead organic seven grain cereal (wheat-free) that is cooked. It is mixed with a little rice milk and a slice of banana. A few hulled sesame seeds and crushed egg shells (boiled twenty minutes and dried) are sprinkled on top. It is served once a week. Sometimes they are given bits of scrambled or hard-boiled egg on alternative days.

✔ **A mash diet** is served daily. I purchase an array of fresh, organic fruits, vegetables, legumes, and grains from the grocery store. Then I create the mash daily. First, the items are soaked in water, with a little apple cider vinegar to wash off any dirt and pesticides. They are rinsed and dried. I cut them into bits. Then I grate them in a mini food processor.

• There are at least ten vegetables in the concoction. This always includes a small portion of a leaf from at least two green leafy vegetables (examples are mustard greens, chard, chicory, collards, kale, beet greens, and so on). Vegetables chosen for the week depend on what is fresh. Examples include: red pepper, corn, broccoli, carrots, peas, grape tomatoes, okra, yellow squash, asparagus, and so on.

• Other ingredients, such as a half spoon portion of cooked basmati brown rice and an assortment of cooked beans, are added to the concoction.

• To make the mash more alluring, I add either one small organic strawberry or a squirt from an organic juice orange slice to sweeten. I also finely chop a slice of apple in each bird's bowl or finely grate a "fingernail" portion of low-fat cheese that is mixed with the mash in the bowl. The apple and cheese are served only a few times per week. They are mixed with the mash so that my parrots get the benefit of the other ingredients while seeking out the goodies.

✔ **A dry foods bowl** is served daily. Ingredients consist of pellets, one or two peanuts, pumpkin seeds, hulled sesame seeds, pine nuts, crushed egg shells, almonds, and dry cereal. Mineral supplements are sprinkled on them.

✔ **A late afternoon snack** is served, consisting of their favorite fruits, such as cantaloupe, grapes, and berries.

✔ **Dinner time** consists of a spoonfeeding of a pureed food. This is given a few times per week (see the Pureed Food, page 74). We also share tiny portions of dinner (such as bits of a vegetable/rice medley). Finally, at the end of

CHECKLIST

Food No/No's
✘ Avocado
✘ Caffeine
✘ Chocolate
✘ Rhubarb
✘ Carbonated beverages
✘ Pits, seeds of many fruits
✘ Alcoholic beverages
✘ High-fat, fried, and salty foods
✘ High sugar foods
✘ Chemical preservatives and dyes
✘ Artificial coloring and flavoring
✘ Any item you feel nervous about, do not serve.

the day, we enjoy our evening snack. This includes a half tablespoon of sunflower seeds for them and low-fat yogurt for me (sometimes also for them).

[1]McWatters, Alicia, Ph.D., C.N.C., *A Guide to a Naturally Healthy Parrot.* Safe Goods Publishing, East Canaan, Connecticut, 1997, pp. 2–3.

[2]McWatters, Alicia, Ph.D., C.N.C., "Are Sunflower Seeds for the Birds?" *Grey Play Round Table.* Tewillager Publishing, division of Equatorial Group, Ltd., Old Chatham, New York, Summer 1997, p. 15.

[3]McWatters, Alicia, Ph.D., C.N.C., *A Guide to a Naturally Healthy Parrot,* Safe Goods Publishing, East Canaan, Connecticut, 1997, pp. 31–32.

THE VETERINARY EXPERIENCE

It is scary to be wrapped up, poked, and prodded in a veterinary exam. Some greys have become terrorized, and have even turned phobic, after rough, obtrusive experiences.
A concerned veterinarian with a gentle style can make a difference. In addition to technical skill, it is important to find an avian veterinarian who can establish a rapport with your grey.

Choosing the Right Veterinarian

✔ Does he/she have experience helping greys?
✔ Does he/she have a good rapport with your parrot?
✔ How is the facility staffed? Does it have state-of-the-art equipment?
✔ Is the veterinarian the primary caregiver, instead of a staff member?
✔ Does he/she answer your questions satisfactorily? Does he/she return your phone calls?
✔ Does he/she have a good reputation/track record of helping parrots in the bird community?
✔ Is the facility appropriately staffed to handle emergencies, even in the middle of the night and on holidays?

Your grey's health is your responsibility.

✔ Is the veterinarian a member of the Association of Avian Veterinarians, and does he/she continually update him/herself on new findings?
Tip: When the veterinarian first enters the exam room, introduce your bird to him or her. If the visit is not an emergency, spend a few minutes talking about some of your parrot's favorite games or phrases. Let your bird show off. Then tell your grey what the veterinarian will do. Explain that the vet is gentle and will not harm it. Request the bird to "step up" from your hand onto the veterinarian's hand. Encourage the veterinarian to play with your bird briefly before commencing the exam.

What to Expect in a Health Exam

Bring your parrot to the veterinarian's office in a safe carrier. Carry along fresh samples of poop, as well as any past medical records or detailed notes of observations and questions you may have. If you plan to have your grey's wings and nails clipped, bring along scissors (such as bandage scissors without sharp points) and a nail file. If the veterinarian's equipment is sterilized between exams, his or her clipping equipment is also acceptable. However, it is always advised to bring along a towel that is designated only for your parrot. "New bird" exams and quarantine measures are discussed in Before Bringing Your Grey Home.

After the "getting acquainted period," the veterinarian will conduct a physical work-up. First, your parrot will be toweled. Then an assistant will hold the parrot, while the veterinarian examines its head, eyes, ears, beak, throat, abdomen, under wings, feathers, legs, feet, and so on.

Tip: Toweling can be a grueling experience. If you are good at toweling your grey, do it yourself. Then hand the parrot over to the veterinarian and assistant. A good veterinarian is constantly analyzing your bird's reactions and identifying ways to make the experience as easy as possible. My greys' veterinarian discovered that they were calmer if she turned out the lights before toweling them.

TIP

Immediate Action

Birds are known for their rapid decline in health when early symptoms of illness are left untreated or go undetected. Therefore, you should treat any of the early warning signs as a medical emergency for which an immediate trip to your avian veterinarian is warranted.

Various laboratory tests may be conducted, including:

A fecal (poop) exam determines potential presence of intestinal parasites.

A Gram stain test is conducted on fecal matter and any identified discharges to evaluate the presence of bacteria and fungus.

Cultures and sensitivities testing are conducted if there is a presence of bacteria or fungus. It helps determine the most appropriate medication, if needed.

A complete blood count (CBC) analyzes the white and red blood cell count.

A blood chemistry profile can give you an overview of your parrot's health, including an overview of nutrient deficiencies in the body.

There are some potential illnesses that can affect African greys; therefore, your veterinarian may recommend testing for a few of them.

Psittacosis is caused by the *Chlamydia psittaci* bacteria. It is easily curable when detected early in parrots. It can be transferred to humans and is potentially dangerous to those with compromised immune systems. It acts like a virus causing flulike symptoms.

Psittacine Beak and Feather Disease (PBFD) is a virus that attacks the immune system. It is very contagious, particularly for young parrots. PBFD results in abnormal beak and feathers that look unhealthy and brittle. Tests to detect the disease, as well as a vaccine, have been developed by Dr. Branson Ritchie of the University of Georgia.

Ployomavirus can be highly contagious and wipe out an entire aviary of baby chicks. According to Dr. Tammy Parker, the illness is so devastating because it lacks early warning signs. It can be spread by feather and fecal dust. Dr. Branson Ritchie's medical group at the

University of Georgia has created tests to detect the disease, in addition to a vaccine.

Tip: You are responsible for the ultimate health of your bird. If you feel uncomfortable about a procedure recommended by your veterinarian, seek other professional opinions.

Early Warning Signs

If a wild flock detects illness in one of its members, it will expel that individual from the group. That's because predators attack sick birds first (easier prey). Therefore, wild birds tend to mask their illnesses from the rest of the flock to avoid being abandoned and left to fend for themselves. Accordingly, in the home, companion parrots instinctively attempt to hide any health problems from us (the flock). By the time sickness becomes obvious, the parrot is usually quite ill. However, regular annual or bi-annual health check-ups can help to detect any potential health problems before they become detrimental.

Weight-loss is one sure sign of a parrot with a potential upcoming illness. Purchase an electronic gram scale. Weigh your African grey a few times per week, always at the same time. Another way to detect weight-loss is to feel along your parrot's keel bone. If it appears to be more prominent than in the past, your bird may be losing weight. If your parrot's weight-

CHECKLIST

Home First Aid Kit
✔ Corn starch, styptic powder
✔ Scissors
✔ Hemostats or fine needle nose pliers
✔ Gauze
✔ Peroxide
✔ Pedialyte
✔ Towel
✔ Small carrier for transport and emergency housing

loss is accompanied by some of the other symptoms listed below, contact your avian veterinarian immediately.

Sudden listlessness and other uncharacteristic activity, such as sleeping when it normally does not, being quiet when normally vocal, and not eating.

Regurgitating for long periods, which could be vomiting.

Sneezing with discharge.

Fluffed up feathers all the time.

Excessive head bobbing and shaking.

Abnormal looking feathers.

Falling off perch and huddling at bottom of cage.

Top left: Turn foods like carrots into toys.

Bottom left: Greys instinctively attempt to hide health problems from the flock.

Top right: Look for a veterinarian who will establish a rapport with your parrot.

Bottom right: Be observant of your grey's behavior.

Top: Healthy greys have clear eyes and nostrils.

Bottom left: A secure African grey is a happy grey.

Bottom right: Active greys need a variety of toys.

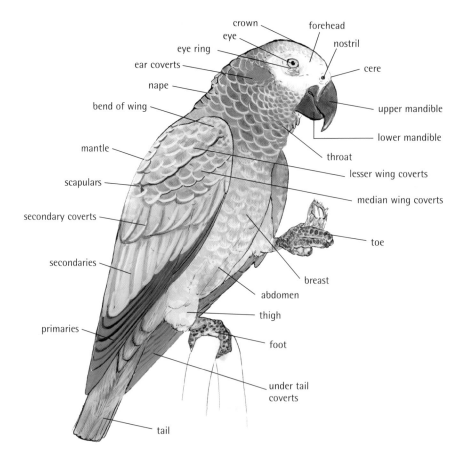

crown forehead
eye nostril
eye ring
ear coverts cere
nape
bend of wing upper mandible
mantle lower mandible
scapulars throat
secondary coverts lesser wing coverts
median wing coverts
secondaries toe
breast
abdomen
thigh
primaries foot
under tail coverts
tail

African grey parrot anatomy.

A Brief Recap

Your African grey's trips to the veterinarian need not be an experience in terror. Examinations by an avian veterinarian should be as unobtrusive as possible.

✔ Choose the right veterinarian. Do some preliminary investigation of local avian veterinarians. Be sure to ask yourself the right questions.

✔ Know what to expect during the course of an examination.

✔ Be aware of the early warning signs of illness in your African grey.

✔ Always have a home first aid kit prepared and well-stocked with clean materials.

✔ Be prepared for emergencies and know how to react properly. See HOW-TO: Emergencies, pages 90–91.

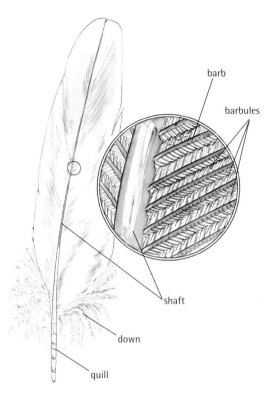

Tiny filaments called barbules link the barbs that come off the central feather shaft or rachis.

Home Hazards

African greys are often killed or injured in household accidents. Listed below are some of the most common causes of death or injury within the home.

✔ Food poisoning. See Food No/No's on page 79 for a detailed list of harmful foods and liquids.

✔ Chemical pesticides, insecticides, and cleaning solvents.

✔ Toxic fumes including secondhand smoke, burning rubber or plastic, and nonstick cooking utensils (Teflon). See page 23.

✔ Toxic plants. See page 23 for a detailed listing.

✔ Poorly designed cages.

✔ Other family pets.

✔ Sliding glass doors.

✔ Open windows and doors.

✔ Standing water such as sinks, toilets, bathtubs, and aquariums.

✔ Electrical cords.

Feathers and Trimming

African greys start to molt their wing feathers at about one year of age. As feathers become longer, especially wing feathers, trimming will become part of any grooming routine. Trimming of the wing feathers is particularly important to your grey's safety. Speak to your veterinarian about the options available to you.

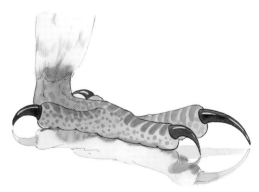

Trim any toenail that lifts the end of the toe off a flat surface. If you are unsure about how to properly trim your grey's toenails, ask your avian veterinarian for help.

Make sure that all toys offered to your African grey are safe. They should be made of nontoxic material, appropriately sized, and properly inspected.

Top: Greys should be fed a balanced diet in order to maintain their optimal health.

Bottom left: A healthy grey is a happy grey.

Bottom right: Healthy treats like millet sprays should be offered in moderation.

Nothing can be more devastating than to have something happen to your cherished companion and being unprepared for it. Emergencies do happen. The first step is to **stay calm** because the more upset you get, the more stressed your parrot will become. Also:

✔ Keep a list of emergency phone numbers at your finger tips.

✔ Keep a travel carrier at your door for quick evacuation.

✔ Keep a first-aid kit on hand and update periodically.

✔ Keep at least three days of food and water on hand. This includes favorite dried foods, such as seeds and fruits, that your parrot will eat, no matter the circumstances.

✔ Keep the following supplies on hand: flashlight/batteries, nonscented candles/matches, portable radio/batteries, disinfectant/bleach, blankets for warmth and covering cages.

Beak Bleeding

Parrots' beaks contain blood vessels. A beak break can result in heavy bleeding. If your grey breaks its beak, remain calm. Place the bird on a perch and look at the beak to determine the area and extent of damage. Rinse the beak with hydrogen peroxide. Then fill a dish with either corn starch or flour. Dip the beak in the dish and pad. Continue until the bleeding stops. Once the bleeding stops, make an immediate appointment with the veterinarian. Sometimes accidents cause slight fractures that look like faint lines. The veterinarian needs to determine the full extent of the problem.

Your bird's beak will be sore over the next few days, and it may be difficult for it to eat. Therefore, observe how much it eats and supplement its diet by spoon feeding pureed foods, until your parrot is eating normally.

Animal Bites

Dog and cat bites can cause severe shock and possibly death, if the parrot is not

Dip the beak in the dish and pad.

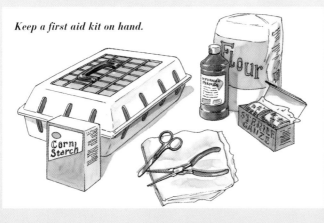

Keep a first aid kit on hand.

taken to the veterinarian immediately. Even a scratch can cause death in a matter of hours. Flush the wound with a gentle saline solution (such as contact lens saline solution). Apply pressure to the wound. Rush to the nearest animal emergency center.

Blood Feathers

A blood feather is a feather that is growing and continues to receive a blood supply. Sometimes they are sticking out of the wing. Also, if your parrot has a nervous, flapping incident in the cage, it may damage a blood feather. A damaged blood feather will bleed profusely until it is totally pulled out. Clamp it with either tweezers or needle-nose pliers and gently pull the feather straight out. If the follicle continues to bleed after the feather is removed, apply pressure for a few minutes. You may also pad the area with cornstarch or styptic powder.

Heatstroke

Heatstroke occurs when your parrot has been in a hot place, such as in the sun without shade or in a hot car. Its body temperature can get to dangerous levels. If it is panting and holding its wings away from its body, immediately move it to a cool place. Spray its body with water. Place its feet in a bowl of cool water or rub water on its feet while holding it. Give it either water or pedialyte to drink.

Toxic Fumes

If you notice your parrot panting from toxic fumes, such as PTFE poisoning or scented candles (see Teaching Your Grey Everyday Living

Clamp the blood feather and gently pull it straight out.

Skills), remove it from the area as quickly as possible. Immediately open a window. Sit calmly with the bird near the window. Then rush the parrot to the nearest animal emergency center.

Sit calmly with the bird near an opened screened window. Never leave a bird unattended.

Organizations

The African Parrot Society
P.O. Box 204
Clarinda, Iowa 51632-2731

American Federation of Aviculture (AFA)
P.O. Box 56218
Phoenix, Arizona 85079-6218

Association of Avian Veterinarians
(561) 393-8901

Bird Clubs of America
P.O. Box 280383
Memphis, Tennessee 38168

Canadian Parrot Association
32 Dronmore Court
Willowdale, Ontario
M2R 2H5
Canada

The Gabriel Foundation
P.O. Box 11477
Aspen, Colorado 81612

International Aviculturists Society (IAS)
P.O. Box 2232
LaBelle, Florida 33975

Oasis Parrot Sanctuary
P.O. Box 3104
Scottsdale, Arizona 85271

Parrot Rehabilitation Society
P.O. Box 620213
San Diego, California 92102-0213

The World Parrot Trust
P.O. Box 34114
Memphis, Tennessee 38184

Periodicals

Bird Talk (Monthly)
P.O. Box 57347
Boulder, Colorado 80323-7347

Wild Congo greys are partial ground feeders (Bolou Savanna, Lobéké Reserve, Cameroon).

Grey Play Round Table (Quarterly)
P.O. Box 190
Old Chatham, New York 12136
http://www.africangreys.com
(specifically for grey owners)

Original Flying Machine (Bimonthly)
10645 North Tatum Boulevard, Suite 200, #459
Phoenix, Arizona 85028-3053

Pet Bird Report (Bimonthly)
2236 Mariner Square Drive #35
Alameda, California 94501-6745

Books

Bergman, Petra. *Feeding Your Pet Bird.* Hauppauge, New York: Barron's Educational Series, Inc., 1993.

Forshaw, Joseph M. *Parrots of the World.* Neptune, New Jersey: T.F.H. Publications Inc., 1977.

Gonzales, Fran. *African Greys.* Yorba Linda, California: Neon Pet Publications, 1996.

Juniper, Tony, and Parr, Mike. *Parrots: A Guide to Parrots of the World.* New Haven, Connecticut: Yale University Press, 1998.

McWatters, Alicia. *A Guide to a Naturally Healthy Bird.* 1997. To order, contact: (505) 281-5168.

Pepperberg, Irene M. *The Alex Studies.* Boston, Massachusetts: Harvard University Press, 2000.

Short, Lester L. *The Lives of Birds.* New York, New York: Henry Holt and Company, 1993.

Photo Credits

Joan Balzarini: pages 3, 4, 5, 8, 12, 13, 16, 17, 20 top left, 20 top right, 21 top left, 24 top left, 24 top right, 24 bottom, 25 bottom left, 25 bottom right, 28, 29, 32, 33 top, 33 bottom, 36, 37, 41, 44 top, 45, 52, 53, 56 top, 57, 60, 61 top, 61 bottom, 65, 68 top left, 68 top right, 68 bottom, 69 top left, 69 top right, 69 bottom, 73, 76 top left, 76 top right, 76 bottom, 77 top left, 77 top right, 77 bottom, 80, 81, 84 top left, 84 top right, 84 bottom left, 84 bottom right, 85 top, 85 bottom right, 88 top left, 88 top right, 88 bottom left, 89 top, 89 bottom left, 89 bottom right, 93 top, 93 bottom; Diana L. May: pages 9, 92; Carole D. Ward: page 21 top right; Barbara Reilly: page 20 bottom; Susan Briggs: pages 25 top, 56 bottom; Paulette Jacob: pages 40, 72; J.C. Van Brederode: page 44 bottom; Theresa Gardian: page 64; Penny M. Panculias: page 85 bottom left.

Cover Credits

All cover photography by Joan Balzarini.

Important Note

The subject of this book is how to take care of African grey parrots in captivity. In dealing with these birds, always remember that newly purchased birds—even when they appear perfectly healthy—may well be carriers of transmittable diseases. This is why it is highly advisable to have sample droppings analyzed and to observe strict hygienic rules. Other infectious diseases that can endanger humans are rare in African greys. However, if you see a doctor because you or a member of your household has symptoms of a cold or the flu, mention that you keep birds.

No one who is allergic to feathers or feather dust should keep birds. If you have any doubts, consult your physician before you buy a bird.

About the Author

Maggie Wright has been working with African greys since the early nineties. She is the creator, publisher, and editor for the grey magazine, *The Grey Play Round Table*. She has also contributed articles to other magazines in the United States and Europe, including *Bird Talk, The Original Flying Machine,* and *The Pet Bird Report.* Maggie shares her life with two Congo greys, Merlin Tewillager and Sweet Pea.

All inquiries should be addressed to:
Barron's Educational Series, Inc.
250 Wireless Boulevard
Hauppauge, NY 11788
http://www.barronseduc.com

International Standard Book No. 0-7641-1035-7

Library of Congress Catalog Card No. 00-050788

Library of Congress Cataloging-in-Publication Data
Wright, Margaret T.
    African grey parrots : a complete pet owner's manual : everything about purchase, care, nutrition, behavior, and training / Margaret T. Wright.
        p. cm.
    Includes bibliographical references (p.).
    ISBN 0-7641-1035-7 (alk. paper)
    1. African grey parrot. I. Title.
SF473.P3 W75   2001
636.6'865—dc21   00-050788

Printed in China

9 8